As the Co-Founder and CEO of CBT News, I've witnessing some of the best minds in the retail automotive industry, and Adam Marburger stands out among them. His extraordinary talent, sharp strategic mind, and unwavering integrity make him a true leader in F&I training. Through Ascent Dealer Services, Adam has consistently raised the bar, empowering dealerships and inspiring professionals to excel. His impact on the industry is nothing short of transformative.

— **Jim Fitzpatrick,**
Co-Founder and CEO | JBF Business Media

Adam Marburger isn't just a leader; he's a force of nature—an innovator, a mentor, and a once-in-a-generation trailblazer who proves that with vision and grit, the road to greatness is paved with service to others. A black belt in both martial arts and F&I, Adam embodies both servant leadership and the entrepreneurial spirit that fuels innovation. Through his strategic mindset and unwavering humility, he has empowered countless dealers to drive profitability and achieve sustainable growth. In this book, Adam shares the principles and practices that helped him build two of the fastest-growing companies in their industries, revolutionize dealership operations, and inspire others to reach their full potential. This book is a roadmap for anyone seeking to lead with purpose, adapt to challenges, and leave a lasting impact.

— **Joe St. John,**
Chief Customer Officer | AutoFi

Adam Marburger is one of the most formidable leaders I have had the pleasure of knowing. In my years of working alongside industry leaders, few stand out as distinctly as Adam. His unapologetic drive for excellence, paired with a relentless determination to stay at the top, is a testament to his personal drive to succeed regardless of obstacles. What sets Adam apart, however, is not just his personal success, but his unwavering commitment to lifting others along the way. His leadership philosophy is clear: success is not a solitary achievement but one that is shared and celebrated with those around him. Adam's ability to inspire and empower those around him is nothing short of extraordinary.

— **Shannon Robertson,**
Executive Director | AFIP

Passion, Process, Performance. When others try to create scripts, Adam has created an F&I buying experience that has successfully transformed hundreds of dealerships to serve their customers and speed up the process at the same time. No tricks, no gimmicks, the future is now, and Adam brings it to you!

— **Adam Arens,**
Dealer Principal | Patriot Auto Group

I've known and worked with Adam for over 20 years. He's driven by passion and successful from persistence. Building a business isn't for the weak; it takes mental strength, integrity, and dedication. These are the three components that best explain how Adam is built. Anyone who does business with him or is fortunate enough to call him a friend, like me, is better for it.

— **Craig Schmitz,**
Dealer Principal | Auto Centers Nissan

Adam is a remarkable individual whose charisma and insight shine through in his latest book, "The Servant Leading F&I Manager: Leadership Refined." His writing ability reflects a deep understanding of the dynamics of leadership, inspiration, and finance, seamlessly blending personal anecdotes with practical strategies. Adam's approach to servant leadership emphasizes empathy and collaboration, making complex concepts accessible to readers. His dedication to empowering others is evident not only in his words but also in his commitment to cultivating strong relationships, both in writing and life. This book is a testament to his passion for helping others succeed in their professional journeys.

— **Stan Qualls,**
GM / Director of Operations | Seelye Auto Group

THE SERVANT LEADING F&I MANAGER:

LEADERSHIP REDEFINED

ADAM MARBURGER

Photographer: AJ Stotler

ISBN: 978-1-966840-00-8

To Bill Haegele,

This book is dedicated to you, my friend and former boss, who believed in me even when I struggled to believe in myself. Promoting me to F&I Manager at the young age of 22 was a pivotal moment in my life, and I will forever be grateful for your trust and support.

Your unwavering respect and kindness created an environment where I could grow and thrive. You were not only a brilliant operator with an exceptional understanding of the automotive industry but also a remarkable human being who mentored countless individuals, leaving a lasting impact on all who had the privilege of knowing you.

Though we lost you this past summer, your legacy continues to inspire me and so many others. The world is undoubtedly a better place because of your contributions, and I can confidently say that I am a better person because of the lessons I learned from you.

Thank you for everything, Bill. Your influence will forever resonate in my heart and in these pages.

ACKNOWLEDGMENTS

I have far too many people to thank and, unfortunately, not enough space to name them all. To everyone I've had the privilege of working with throughout my time as a retail F&I professional—thank you. I am sincerely grateful to all the bank reps, buyers, funders, sales associates, F&I Managers, desk managers, service writers, office staff, and, of course, the customers I've served. This journey has been nothing short of extraordinary.

A special thank you to Craig Schmitz. Craig, you are the owner of the dealership where I spent nearly 15 years of my life. You taught me how to lead and showed me what it takes to succeed. You've always had my back and pushed me to embrace entrepreneurship, even when I wasn't sure I was ready. You've been an incredible mentor, always willing to take my calls—even when my ideas were out there. Without you, I wouldn't be where I am today. Thank you.

To Johnny Garlich—Johnny, you are the reason I entered the world of F&I products and reinsurance. You were my agent throughout my retail career, always there to guide and support me. When I left retail, you took me under your wing and showed me the ropes of becoming an F&I product agent. You are, without question, the most brilliant man I've ever met, and I'm endlessly grateful for your mentorship and friendship.

These individuals were instrumental in shaping my career in retail automotive. My promise to them is to lead the younger generation with the same care and guidance they showed me. It's so important to acknowledge those who paved the way for us and to pay it forward by helping others. Thank you all for everything. This journey has been special, and I look forward to what's ahead.

Lastly, to my incredible team at Ascent Dealer Services, I am profoundly thankful to be surrounded by people who inspire and motivate me every single day. Their dedication, drive, and passion are unmatched, and they constantly push me to become the best version of myself.

Through servant leadership and a relentless commitment to serving others, we have grown into one of the most respected and sought-after F&I providers in the automotive industry. This level of success didn't happen by accident—it's the result of assembling a dream team of professional coaches who work tirelessly to serve our dealer clients and help them achieve next-level growth.

One of the greatest lessons I've learned is to hire people who are smarter than me, trust them, and empower them to lead with excellence. This team embodies that philosophy, and because of them, Ascent Dealer Services is more than just a company—it's a family dedicated to making a lasting impact on our industry. I am deeply grateful for their hard work, their heart for service, and their shared vision of excellence. Together, we are unstoppable.

CONTENTS

FOREWORD

The Black Belt of Leadership: A Secret Weapon

Really? You are reading the Foreword?? What's the matter with you? And not just that, the foreword of yet ANOTHER leadership book? From a black belt in leadership, no less?

What can be said about leadership that hasn't already been written, said, or quoted? You may even be thinking that the world needs another leadership book like politicians need to write more laws and policies.

And what about leadership in automotive? Is that even a thing?

Let's be honest: the average dealership manager was promoted into that role because the last one was fired or quit.

Our industry is filled with dealers and managers who don't care about leadership, about developing others, let alone themselves—or at least many don't!

AND THAT IS WHY YOU SHOULD READ THIS BOOK.

You see, the attitude above is the exact attitude of 90% of your competitors. The dealership down the road, across town, and the one your next client will compare you to is likely being managed by people who subscribe to that exact kind of limited mindset. Many still think leadership is a competition of who can yell the loudest, talk down to people, or make themselves more important by making others less important!

But not you!

You are reading this book because you are different. This book is different because it is written by a respected and experienced leader in our industry who not only leads his team to record-breaking growth, but he does so with integrity of character!

I know you are different than other leaders and managers!

How do I know you are different?

Because in my capacity as a consultant and trainer, I've personally been in over 3,000 dealerships, across 7 countries and 3 continents. I also have the honor of being a 24-time NADA speaker and consultant to many of the top dealerships in the country, along with being the personal coach to some of the best salespeople to ever sell cars!

All that means I have seen more than most, and one thing that my 20+ years of experience has given me is perspective!

So, when Adam Marburger said, "I'm going to write a book about servant leadership," I immediately knew two things: Number one, it needed to be written for people like you who need the encouragement, reminders, strategies, and practical applications! And secondly, it needed to be written by Adam—someone who serves from the heart, lives with conviction, and whose twenty years of commitment and dedication to our industry has demonstrated the delicate and deliberate duality of serving and leading!

You are a servant leader, too. I can tell. You wouldn't be determined to read this book if you didn't have the heart of a servant and the vision of a leader!

In this book, you will be inspired by the stories, challenged by the strategies, and determined to implement the tactical and practical ways that Adam shows us how to live out the lifestyle of leadership.

In closing, I want to let you know that I'm truly excited for you! I'm excited for the changes that will begin in you and then begin to impact your family, friends, coworkers, and community.

What are we, except the collection of ideas, habits, and beliefs that we live out daily? Anytime you intentionally rewrite your brain, you change your future! That's what you are doing RIGHT NOW!

I can already imagine how this book will be a resource you and your team will come back to again and again!

Lastly, I encourage you to share this journey with someone! Whether it's by gifting a copy to some members of your team, or by simply sharing quotes and inspirations this book challenges you with. Whatever that looks like for you, I invite you to serve others as you learn how to lead others with Servant Leadership!

Jonathan W. Dawson

President, LITE Consulting, Inc.

Founder, Sellchology - Selling thru Psychology

Co-Founder, Pinnacle Society

PREFACE

I wrote this book for us—the automotive professionals who strive to make an impact in this world. It has been an incredible privilege to work alongside two exceptional dealer groups near St. Louis, Missouri. Over the course of my career, I had the opportunity to complete more than 20,000 retail F&I transactions. In 2017, my mentor, Johnny Garlich, presented me with the chance to scale my impact from one rooftop to a national stage. Taking that leap into the unknown was daunting, but it was one of the best decisions of my life, and I am forever grateful.

The automotive industry has been nothing short of a blessing for my family and me. It has allowed me to dedicate my days to helping dealers improve their F&I operations, and it has provided a fulfilling career in an ever-evolving field. Automotive professionals are a rare breed—when challenges arise, we find solutions. I'm proud of what we accomplish as a collective force. We don't just sell cars; we provide vital transportation solutions for our customers while creating meaningful careers for ourselves.

This book is a reflection of over two decades in the retail automotive world. It's meant to be a resource for personal and professional growth, a guide to help you become more self-aware and motivated to reach your highest potential. We live in a country brimming with opportunities, and the automotive industry offers more possibilities than any other field I've encountered.

Let me be upfront—I'm a proud college dropout. Today, I own and operate seven successful companies, including Ascent Dealer Services, one of the most relevant F&I companies in the business. I don't share this to boast but to emphasize that with hard work, a commitment to personal development, and a relentless drive, you can achieve incredible results. This industry rewards those who dedicate themselves, and the possibilities are endless if you commit to self-mastery.

Often, we're so caught up in distractions that we fail to see the opportunities right in front of us. Never doubt that you can achieve more—there is always another level to reach. If you dedicate yourself to growth, both personally and professionally, you will continue to ascend.

This book is here to enhance your F&I skills, improve the buying experience for your customers, and help you lead effectively in your dealership and personal life.

I'll leave you with one ask: As you grow, extend a hand to the younger generation. They're watching us—their leaders in the automotive industry. Let's set the standard, lead by example, and always approach leadership with a servant's heart. Leadership is a privilege, and our work is never truly done. Thank you for taking the time to read this book. Investing in yourself is the best decision you can make. You deserve to become the best version of yourself. Let's get started.

SECTION 1:
Personal Foundations of Leadership

CHAPTER 1:
Paperboy Turned Sales Professional

In the quiet town of Wood River, Illinois, nestled between the hustle of everyday life, my journey into the world of sales began in an unexpected place—a paper route. Growing up in a middle-class family, I learned the values of hard work and determination from an early age. My father, a dedicated shift worker at the local oil refinery, and my mother, a diligent paralegal, instilled in my brother and me the importance of earning what we wished for in life.

We didn't have the luxury of new Jordans or shiny new cars waiting for us on our sixteenth birthdays. Instead, we were taught to roll up our sleeves and put in the effort. That mindset laid the foundation for everything I would later accomplish in my career.

At just thirteen years old, I took my first step into the world of sales with the *Alton Telegraph*. My paper route was more than a job; it became my first lesson in responsibility, customer service, and even servant leadership. Each morning, I would rise at 5:30 am, prepare the newspapers with precision, and set out on my bike, Walkman headphones in place, delivering the day's news. While the delivery itself taught discipline, it was the monthly subscription collections that taught me the art of sales. Wages were minimal, so tips were key. It required interaction, persuasion, and trust. I learned to engage customers with sincerity, asking questions like, "Was your paper delivered on time? Was it rolled properly? Did it stay dry when it rained?"

Those small moments of service built a relationship, one that often ended with me making a heartfelt pitch: "This paper route is how I'm saving for my first car. If I've done a good job, I'd appreciate your support."

Those early lessons in creating value and building trust turned into generous tips and a sense of accomplishment. My work ethic caught the attention of the *Alton Telegraph*, and I was awarded two additional routes by the time I turned sixteen. Looking back, that small paper route wasn't just a job; it was the first stepping stone on my journey as a servant leader in sales.

Summary

This chapter recounts my earliest experiences in sales and how a simple paper route laid the foundation for a career built on responsibility, trust, and servant leadership. By sharing this story, I aim to show that even small beginnings can lead to significant success when approached with diligence and a heart for service.

Key Takeaways

1. **Servant Leadership Starts Early:** Even in seemingly small roles, leading with service and integrity creates a foundation for long-term success.
2. **Relationships Matter:** Building trust and genuinely caring for others turns simple transactions into meaningful connections.
3. **Hard Work Pays Off:** The discipline and effort invested in early experiences often pave the way for greater opportunities.

Action Steps

1. **Reflect on Your Start:** Think about your first job or role—what lessons did it teach you about responsibility and service? Write down three takeaways that still influence you today.
2. **Prioritize Service:** In your current role, identify one way to go above and beyond for a customer, colleague, or team member. Act on it this week.
3. **Revisit the Basics:** Identify a current task or responsibility that seems routine. Approach it with fresh eyes, focusing on how you can add value to others.

Use this story as inspiration to approach every interaction with the mindset of a servant leader. Even in high-pressure roles, focus on serving the customers and building trust.

For Teams

Share your personal journey with your team to inspire them to see value in their work, no matter their role.

For Personal Growth

Reflect on the foundational lessons in your career and consider how they still apply to your daily life. Use these insights to refine your approach to leadership and service.

Bridging Reflection to Action

The values I learned as a paperboy—service, trust, and hard work—became the cornerstone of my approach to leadership. No matter where you began, those early lessons hold the power to shape how you lead and serve today. Take a moment to reflect: How can you apply those foundational principles to your current role?

In Chapter 2, we'll explore how adversity can become a catalyst for transformation, pushing us to grow, lead with purpose, and embrace resilience.

CHAPTER 2:
Ignorant Decisions Don't Define You

"Our greatest glory is not in never falling, but in rising every time we fall." — Confucius

Sometimes, it takes hitting rock bottom to recognize the path to growth and purpose. In the summer of 1999, one decision changed everything for me—a moment that would ultimately ignite a journey of resilience, self-discovery, and servant leadership.

In the summer of 1999, I found myself suspended in the air, a helicopter slicing through the clouds above Wood River, Illinois. My life hung in the balance, a direct result of a poor choice influenced by a so-called friend and a drug called liquid G. What happened next was a blur of sirens and panic, culminating in a moment of clarity when my little brother Brent discovered me and called for help.

When I awoke, the weight of my actions crashed over me like a tidal wave. There, in that cold hospital room, I heard a whisper—a gentle reminder that, by the grace of God, I had been granted another chance at life. At just 18 years old, I was a punk kid who had danced on the edge of oblivion and somehow stumbled back. Disappointment in myself mingled with flickers of hope, igniting a spark deep within.

The Turning Point

This near-death experience led me to search for God and attempt to turn my life around. I felt different when I woke up in that hospital bed—safe, loved, and aware that I had another chance to change my life. My grandmother was the first person I remember seeing upon waking, and she was understandably upset with me. My family was scared, and I felt like I had let everyone down. Deep down, I knew I was destined for a life much greater than the one I was living. I made a deal with myself in that hospital room to commit to a life of progression, promising to work on myself in all aspects and become a better version of myself each day.

A New Beginning

After the incident, I started hanging out with a group of guys from a rival school in Roxana, Illinois, and one of them, Nick Davenport, became one of my best friends. We spent a lot of time together at the gym and playing sports. A few weeks after my near-death experience, Nick invited me to join his family on a vacation to Panama City Beach. It was an easy "yes" because, at that point, I had only seen the ocean once and had never been to the Gulf of Mexico. I wanted to get away to ponder, reflect, and distance myself from everyone. That trip was unforgettable, and I smile every time I return to Panama City Beach, Florida. It's important to get lost sometimes so you can find yourself, and the beach is a great place to do just that.

Embracing the Automotive Industry

One week later, with amazing memories of perfect weather and beautiful beaches, I returned home only to be met with unexpected news. The restaurant where I had worked was closing, a sudden end to a chapter I had not anticipated. But then came a twist of fate—the owner, a mentor and friend, offered me a lifeline. He wanted to take me to the local Toyota dealership, the very place where he had once thrived as a top salesman.

Initially, I was not interested in this proposition. My mentor, Gordon Carver, was the best salesperson I knew, so he scheduled an interview with the general manager of the dealership and ensured that I showed up. I told the GM that I preferred to work in the service department first, specifically in the detail department, as I was a little intimidated by the idea of selling cars. Mark, the GM, granted my wish, and I was awarded the position of "porter" for $7.50 per hour.

A few weeks into my position in the detail department, I found myself becoming friendly with the sales team. They utilized me for dealer trades and often had me grabbing their lunch. I became close to almost the entire sales staff and spent most of my time outside of the dealership with them. After some time in the detail department, I decided to transition over to the sales department. Let me be clear: I absolutely loved my job in the detail department. I took pride in my work and enjoyed taking old, neglected vehicles and making them look brand new again.

My life transitioned from tragedy to newfound purpose. The automotive industry, often seen as a mere business, became my sanctuary—a place that not only saved my life but transformed it. Through the years, I have witnessed the power of this industry to change lives, to uplift those who dare to dream, and to serve those around us. Whenever someone asks me what I do for a living, I proudly say, "I am a car salesman."

I am very proud of the automotive industry and the opportunities that come with it. I would not be where I am today without following Gordon to his Toyota dealership. I truly believe in my heart that helping individuals with their transportation needs is an honor and a privilege.

A Little More About Me

I worked as a high-volume finance and insurance (F&I) producer for almost two decades, handling over 20,000 retail transactions. I was deeply committed to my dealership, F&I products, fellow staff, and my customers.

In early 2017, I began feeling unfulfilled in my role and sensed that I was meant to coach F&I professionals on a larger scale. The owner of the dealership, Craig Schmitz, was a mentor and dear friend to me. He embraced my decision to venture into the unknown. To this day, he remains one of my biggest supporters, and I spend every Memorial and Labor Day weekend with him at the lake.

Today, I am the president and CEO of one of the largest and most respected F&I companies in the industry, Ascent Dealer Services. We work with some of the most prestigious dealer groups in the industry and have secured healthy OEM partnerships. I have the honor and privilege to speak at NADA, 20 Groups, and stages all over the country. I share this with you for one reason: To encourage you to embrace the automotive industry and fall madly in love with it. There is no other industry like automotive, and your opportunities are endless.

Summary

Ignorant decisions may define moments in our lives, but they don't define who we are. Resilience, self-awareness, and the decision to grow can turn mistakes into transformative turning points. My journey from a near-death experience to becoming a leader in the F&I industry is a testament to the power of second chances and servant leadership. This chapter emphasizes that no matter how challenging the circumstances, you can rewrite your story with commitment, integrity, and humility.

Key Takeaways

1. **Resilience Over Regret:** Mistakes are inevitable; what matters is how you recover and grow from them.
2. **Commitment to Growth:** Personal and professional progressions require daily effort and reflection.
3. **The Power of Mentorship:** Strong mentors and leaders can guide us toward better opportunities and life paths.
4. **Purpose-Driven Leadership**: Transforming challenges into purpose helps you become a more effective leader.
5. **Embrace Humility:** Leadership isn't about perfection—it's about progress and serving others authentically.

Action Steps

For F&I Managers

1. **Evaluate Your Leadership Style:** Reflect on how your personal experiences shape your leadership and interactions with others.
2. **Mentor Proactively:** Look for opportunities to guide newer team members, helping them grow personally and professionally.
3. **Build Resilience:** Develop strategies to navigate challenges with grace, inspiring your team to do the same.
4. **Share Your Story:** Use personal lessons to connect authentically with colleagues and customers.
5. **Commit to Daily Progress:** Set small, achievable goals each day that align with your professional mission.

For Dealership Teams

1. **Foster a Supportive Environment:** Encourage open communication and collaboration among departments to create a unified team.
2. **Value Second Chances:** Recognize potential in others, even if they've made mistakes, and provide guidance to help them improve.

3. **Celebrate Growth:** Highlight team members who exemplify resilience and continuous improvement.
4. **Develop Shared Goals:** Work toward dealership-wide objectives that benefit both the team and the customers.

For Individual Professionals

1. **Reflect on Past Choices:** Identify how past decisions have shaped your journey and what you've learned from them.
2. **Seek Mentorship:** Connect with individuals who can provide valuable guidance and perspective.
3. **Focus on Self-Improvement:** Adopt a mindset of constant learning and development.
4. **Practice Gratitude:** Recognize and appreciate the people and experiences that have contributed to your growth.

How to Apply This

In the F&I Office

Transform past mistakes into teachable moments. Share your lessons learned to foster a culture of authenticity and growth. When presenting F&I products, focus on honesty and integrity, framing each option as a solution rather than a hard sell. Incorporate moments of reflection into your daily routine to ensure alignment with your goals and values.

Across the Dealership

Encourage open dialogue about personal and professional growth during team meetings. Organize mentorship initiatives where experienced team members can guide newer staff. Promote a culture where mistakes are seen as opportunities to learn rather than failures to be punished.

In Your Daily Practice

Dedicate time each day to reflect on your personal progress and goals. Practice active listening during interactions to build genuine connections. Approach challenges with humility and a commitment to finding solutions that serve both the customer and the team.

Practical Tools for Success

As you reflect on this chapter, consider how resilience and growth have shaped your leadership journey. The lessons learned from past mistakes often become the foundation for future success.

Ask Yourself:

1. Personal Practice:
   i. How can I turn my past mistakes into teachable moments for myself and others?
   ii. Am I consistently striving to improve, both personally and professionally?
2. Adaptability:
   i. How do I respond to setbacks or challenges in my career?
   ii. What steps can I take to build resilience within my team or organization?
3. Connection:
   i. How can I use my story to connect authentically with colleagues and customers?
   ii. Am I creating opportunities to support and uplift others around me?
4. Leadership Integrity:
   i. Do my daily actions reflect my commitment to servant leadership?
   ii. How can I create an environment that fosters growth and collaboration?

Bridging Reflection to Action

Reflecting on the challenges and second chances in your own life, think about how these experiences can inspire you to lead with authenticity and purpose. The journey to becoming a servant leader starts with a commitment to personal growth and the willingness to serve others.

CHAPTER 3:

1999 Called and They Want Their Word Tracks Back

"Authenticity is the daily practice of letting go of who we think we're supposed to be and embracing who we are." — Brené Brown

Resilience and adaptability defined the lessons of my early years. These qualities not only saved my life but also shaped how I approached my career. As I transitioned into the automotive industry, I found myself at a crossroads. Much like my personal evolution, the industry was undergoing a transformation of its own—moving away from old transactional practices toward a new era of transparency and trust. This chapter delves into that shift and how we, as leaders, must embrace the change to thrive.

The Shift

As the clock struck midnight on December 31, 1999, the world held its breath, poised on the brink of a new millennium. The 1990s had been a transformative decade, marked by the rise of the internet and a cultural shift that forever altered the landscape of business. Back then, selling was an art form—a dance between the salesperson and the client, often shrouded in mystery. Fast forward to today, and the stage has changed dramatically.

In those earlier days, automotive sales relied heavily on charm, charisma, and, unfortunately, deceit. Salespeople wielded their persuasive skills like a magician with a wand, crafting elaborate pitches designed to captivate and convince. Information was scarce; clients often had to rely on the word of the salesperson alone. This created a dynamic where trust was built through personal relationships but left ample room for miscommunication and misunderstanding.

When I started my career in 1999, I had to endure long hours watching training videos filled with scripted word tracks—forced to memorize lines that felt inauthentic and manipulative. It was brutally painful, yet a condition of my employment. Even then, I knew there had to be a better way to serve customers and meet their needs.

The Evolution of Sales

Today, our clients have evolved. They demand transparency, expecting to know exactly what they are buying, how much it costs, and what the fine print entails. The era of hidden fees and ambiguous terms is fading fast. Clients have access to information at their fingertips, thanks to the internet and social media. A quick search can uncover reviews, comparison prices, and even insights into the sales practices of a company. This knowledge empowers buyers and forces sellers to be upfront about their offerings.

The speed of transaction has also become a crucial factor. In the 1990s, closing a deal could take weeks, if not months. Appointments were scheduled, and follow-ups were often a game of phone tag. Now, the expectation is for swift, seamless transactions. Clients want to make decisions quickly and efficiently without unnecessary delays. The rise of e-commerce has set the standard for speed, and clients now expect that same level of efficiency across all sales channels.

Servant Leadership in Modern Sales

Honesty has emerged as the cornerstone of modern sales. The consequences of deception have never been more pronounced, with social media amplifying the voices of dissatisfied customers. A single negative review can tarnish a company's reputation overnight. Building long-term relationships hinges on authenticity. Clients want to feel valued—not just as a number but as unique individuals with distinct needs.

Reflecting on my own experiences, I remember a time early in my career when I hesitated to take action. I was the problem and the moment I realized that— things started to shift. So many of us are indecisive and are afraid of failure so we never take risks. I will tell you my friends that's not where the good stuff is—take risks!

Summary

The sales tactics of 1999 are relics of a bygone era. To thrive in today's market, we must embrace transparency, speed, and authenticity. Servant leadership—the ability to genuinely listen to clients, understand their needs, and deliver value—has become the foundation of successful sales in the modern age. By focusing on building trust and meaningful connections, we not only elevate the customer experience but also achieve greater success in our careers.

Key Takeaways

1. **Transparency Builds Trust**: Today's customers value honesty over outdated sales tactics. Transparency is non-negotiable in modern sales.
2. **Adaptation Is Essential**: The automotive industry is constantly changing—evolve or risk being left behind.
3. **Customer-Centric Selling Wins**: Focusing on customer needs creates loyalty and repeat business.
4. **Authenticity Over Scripts**: Genuine connections outperform rehearsed word tracks.
5. **Servant Leadership Creates Impact**: Putting customer needs first strengthens your personal and professional brand.

Action Steps

For F&I Managers

1. **Evaluate Your Process**: Review your current approach to ensure transparency and alignment with customer needs.
2. **Engage Early**: Collaborate with the sales team during the initial stages to understand client concerns and preferences.
3. **Educate Yourself**: Stay informed about new trends, products, and customer pain points.
4. **Be Honest About Products**: Clearly outline the benefits and limitations of F&I products without overselling.
5. **Build Long-Term Relationships**: Prioritize customer satisfaction over short-term wins.

For Dealership Teams

1. **Create a Unified Experience**: Collaborate across departments to ensure customers feel valued and understood throughout their journey.

2. **Train Together**: Incorporate team-wide training sessions on transparency and customer engagement.
3. **Celebrate Authenticity**: Reward team members who build authentic customer relationships.

For Individual Professionals

1. **Ditch the Scripts**: Replace rehearsed lines with genuine, customer-focused conversations.
2. **Focus on Listening**: Dedicate time to truly understand what your customers want and need.
3. **Lead with Integrity**: Every interaction should reflect your commitment to serving the customer.
4. **Seek Feedback**: Ask customers and colleagues for feedback on how to improve your approach.

How to Apply This

In the F&I Office

Begin by reviewing your sales process. Identify areas where outdated practices might still exist and replace them with strategies focused on transparency and customer engagement. Train yourself to present F&I products as solutions rather than add-ons.

Across the Dealership

Hold a dealership-wide workshop on the importance of authenticity in modern sales. Use role-playing exercises to help staff identify areas where they can improve their customer interactions. Build processes that reward honesty and collaboration between departments.

In Your Daily Practice

Start each day by reflecting on how you can better serve your customers. During client interactions, focus on active listening and empathy. Follow up after sales to ensure customer satisfaction and build lasting relationships.

Practical Tools for Success

As you reflect on this chapter, consider the transformative journey of the automotive sales profession from the high-pressure, scripted techniques of the past to the authentic, customer-centric approach required today. This evolution mirrors the need for constant adaptation, both in professional and personal spheres. Authenticity and transparency are no longer just ethical ideals—they are practical tools for success.

Ask yourself:

1. **Personal Practice:**
    i. Do I approach my interactions with genuine concern for the client's needs and expectations?
    ii. Are there elements of "word tracks" or outdated habits in my sales process that I should replace with more authentic and flexible approaches?
2. **Adaptability:**
    i. How do I handle the fast-changing expectations of modern customers?
    ii. Am I willing to embrace new technologies and methods to meet client needs more effectively?
3. **Connection:**
    i. Do my interactions build trust and long-term relationships, or do they feel transactional?
    ii. How can I ensure that each client feels valued as an individual rather than just another sale?
4. **Honesty and Integrity:**
    i. In what ways can I reinforce transparency in my communication with clients?
    ii. Am I proactive in addressing potential doubts or misconceptions with honesty?

Bridging Reflection to Action

As you reflect on the principles of authenticity, preparation, and growth, consider how these qualities set the foundation for success. True leadership begins with a willingness to adapt and embrace change, much like the lessons learned in training camp.

In the next chapter, we'll dive deeper into the transformative power of preparation and persistence, exploring how the effort invested behind the scenes shapes the victories we achieve. Just as fights are won in training camp, so too are the foundations of your success as a servant leader in the F&I industry. Let's step into the next phase of your journey—where dedication meets opportunity.

CHAPTER 4:

Fights Are Won in Training Camp

"The fight is won or lost far away from witnesses—behind the lines, in the gym, and out there on the road, long before I dance under those lights." — Muhammad Ali

I have the honor and privilege to speak on stages and work with dealers all over the United States. I start every talk and sales meeting with the same message: Fights are won in training camp.

In the world of professional fighting, the path to victory is paved not in the ring but in the training camp. It's a grueling 12-week journey filled with relentless sparring, intense weight cutting, and sacrifices that test both physical and mental limits. Fighters step into the ring not only to showcase their skills but to demonstrate the culmination of countless hours spent honing their craft, often at the expense of social lives and family time. This dedication is what transforms potential into victory.

I am a black belt in Brazilian Jiu-Jitsu, an 8-time world medalist, national champion, and an undefeated MMA fighter. I'm sharing this with you not to impress you but to impress upon you the importance of training camp. I never won a fight in the ring, cage, or on the mat. It was the time spent in preparation with my team in training camp that led me to victory. The relentless training, the grind, and the sacrifices made all the difference.

As I reflect on my time in the automotive industry, I am reminded of the fierce commitment required of automotive professionals. Just like those fighters, we, too, have our own training camps—our professional development programs, workshops, seminars, and the daily grind of learning and growing within our industry. The effort we invest in our training camp determines our success in the competitive arena of automotive sales and finance.

The Importance of Preparation

In our fast-paced world, the automotive landscape is constantly evolving. New technologies, changing regulations, and shifting consumer expectations require us to stay at the top of our game. Just as a fighter spends weeks perfecting their technique and conditioning their bodies, we must dedicate ourselves to mastering the ever-changing dynamics of our industry. This commitment to personal and professional development is not merely a suggestion; it is essential for our survival and success.

The first step in our training camp is to recognize the need for continuous improvement. As automotive professionals, we must embrace change and adapt to the challenges that come our way. This means seeking out knowledge through formal training programs, mentorship, or simply staying informed about industry trends. Just as fighters study their opponents and analyze their techniques, we must invest time in understanding the market and our competitors to stay ahead.

Resilience in the Face of Challenges

Training camps are not easy; they push fighters to their limits, both physically and mentally. Similarly, our journey in the automotive industry will be fraught with challenges—rejections, difficult clients, and the pressure to meet targets. However, it is during these moments of adversity that we must dig deep and draw upon our training. Resilience is built through experience, and every setback is an opportunity to learn and grow stronger.

When I think about the challenges I faced as an F&I Manager, I remember the long days, the difficult customers, and the pressure to hit performance benchmarks. But it was the preparation—my daily training camp routine—that gave me the resilience to excel in these moments. The lessons learned in preparation became my greatest assets when adversity struck.

The Power of Teamwork

No fighter steps into the ring alone. Fighters rely on coaches, trainers, and teammates to prepare them for battle. In our industry, collaboration is key. Surrounding ourselves with a network of like-minded professionals provides support, inspiration, and accountability.

By sharing insights and strategies, we elevate not only our own performance but that of our colleagues as well.

One of the most valuable lessons I've learned is that the success of any F&I Manager or dealership depends on teamwork. Whether it's the sales team, the service department, or the dealership's leadership, we achieve more when we work together. Building strong relationships with your team is as important as preparing yourself individually.

A Day in the Training Camp

Here is an example of my daily training camp when I was in the F&I office:

1. 5:30 am, rise and shine
2. 5:45 am, prayer-devotion-goals
3. 6:00 am, work out
4. 7:00 am, dress for success
5. 7:15 am, read/study something pertaining to the automotive industry
6. 7:30 am, morning drive on the Great River Road, listening to something motivational
7. 7:45 am, make my way to the dealership
8. 8:00 am, arrive at the dealership
9. 8:05 am, walk service and talk with technicians and service writers
10. 8:10 am, sit and connect with customers in the service waiting lounge
11. 8:20 am, F&I product knowledge training
12. 8:30 am, watch something educational or motivational on YouTube
13. 8:45 am, work on CIT
14. 8:55 am, sit with the sales manager to prepare for the sales meeting
15. 9:00 am, ready to ABSOLUTELY DOMINATE THE DAY

This routine led me to become the highest-performing F&I Manager in the St. Louis market and one of the top producers in the nation. Steve Jobs once said, "The people who are crazy enough to think they can change the world are the ones who do."

Investing in your own training camp will elevate you above your competition. Most F&I Managers show up right on time and are not prepared. Do not be that F&I Manager!

Maintaining Balance

While preparation and resilience are essential, so is maintaining balance. Just as fighters undergo strict regimens, we, too, must manage our work-life balance. The sacrifices made during training camp are significant, but they should not come at the expense of our health or relationships. Finding ways to recharge and reconnect with loved ones is vital to maintaining our motivation and focus.

Embrace the Training Camp Mentality

I urge you to adopt the training camp mentality. Embrace the challenges, commit to ongoing development, and support one another as you navigate your professional journey. The sacrifices you make today, the knowledge you gain, and the resilience you build will prepare you for the victories that await you in the arena of automotive sales and finance. Remember, it's not just about winning the fight; it's about the relentless pursuit of excellence that leads you there.

Alignment with Servant Leadership

Servant leadership thrives on preparation, collaboration, and resilience. As you embrace the training camp mentality, you not only prepare yourself for personal success but also equip yourself to better serve your customers, colleagues, and community. Preparation allows you to be more present, resilient, and supportive of those around you.

Summary

The principle of **training camp** goes beyond professional fighting—it applies directly to our roles as leaders in the automotive industry. Success is determined by the time, effort, and dedication invested in preparation. **Servant leadership**, resilience, teamwork, and continuous improvement are the cornerstones of this approach. By committing to these principles, we create a foundation for excellence, empowering not only ourselves but also our teams and clients.

Key Takeaways

1. **Preparation Leads to Success:** Victory in any field is determined by the effort put in beforehand, not just the execution.
2. **Resilience Is Built Through Challenges:** Adversity is a part of growth; it builds strength and fosters adaptability.
3. **Teamwork Creates Strength:** Collaboration and shared insights elevate collective success.
4. **Consistency Wins the Day:** A disciplined routine, rooted in personal and professional development, drives results.
5. **Servant Leadership Begins in Training:** Preparation equips you to serve your team and clients more effectively.

Action Steps

For F&I Managers

1. **Establish a Daily Routine:** Start your day with intentional practices like study, prayer, and preparation for client interactions.
2. **Engage in Product Knowledge Training:** Dedicate time to understanding your products to present them confidently and authentically.
3. **Create a Feedback Loop:** Regularly review your performance and adjust your strategies for better results.
4. **Mentor New Talent:** Share insights from your own "training camp" with up-and-coming professionals.
5. **Be Ready to Adapt:** Continuously improve to stay ahead of industry trends and client needs.

For Dealership Teams

1. **Collaborate Across Departments:** Build a cohesive "team training camp" to ensure unified customer experiences.
2. **Foster a Culture of Growth:** Encourage team-wide participation in training and knowledge-sharing sessions.
3. **Celebrate Wins Together:** Acknowledge individual and team accomplishments to inspire collective progress.

For Individual Professionals

1. **Dedicate Time to Self-Improvement:** Make learning and development non-negotiable parts of your routine.

2. **Cultivate Resilience:** View challenges as opportunities to strengthen your skills and mindset.
3. **Build Relationships:** Strengthen your network within and outside the dealership to gain support and share insights.
4. **Embrace a Growth Mindset:** Approach each day with a commitment to being better than yesterday.

How to Apply This

In the F&I Office

Develop a morning routine that includes reflection, goal setting, and study. Begin the day by preparing for client interactions with focus and intention. Use training materials and workshops to continuously hone your skills and understanding of your products.

Across the Dealership

Host team training sessions to align goals and strategies. Encourage interdepartmental collaboration to create a seamless customer experience. Leverage mentorship programs to foster growth among team members.

In Your Daily Practice

Adopt a "training camp" mindset by planning each day with purpose and dedicating time to personal growth. Seek feedback to identify areas for improvement and consistently refine your approach. Prioritize building meaningful connections with colleagues and clients.

Practical Tools for Success

As you reflect on this chapter, consider how the principles of preparation, resilience, and teamwork align with servant leadership.

1. **Daily Reflection:** Begin each day with a question—"What can I do today to serve my clients and team better?"
2. **Collaborative Workshops:** Organize training sessions that promote collective learning and accountability.
3. **Personalized Training Camp:** Tailor your routine to include activities that strengthen both professional and personal growth.
4. **Feedback Journals:** Use a journal to track your progress, reflect on challenges, and celebrate victories.

Ask yourself:

1. **Personal Practice:**
   - i. Am I dedicating enough time to prepare myself for success each day?
   - ii. What areas of my routine need improvement or consistency?
2. **Resilience:**
   - i. How do I handle setbacks, and what can I learn from them?
   - ii. Do I have strategies to stay motivated during challenging times?
3. **Teamwork:**
   - i. Am I collaborating effectively with my colleagues to achieve shared goals?
   - ii. How can I better support my team in their own development?
4. **Growth:**
   - i. Am I actively seeking opportunities to grow personally and professionally?
   - ii. What resources or tools could help me achieve my goals?

Bridging Reflection to Action

As we reflect on the commitment, discipline, and preparation required for success, let's connect these principles to the servant leadership journey. The training camp mentality is not just about personal achievement—it's about creating a foundation that allows you to uplift and empower others.

In the next section, we'll explore how to turn this preparation into consistent, impactful leadership that drives results and builds lasting relationships. Let's step into the next phase of your journey with determination and purpose.

SECTION 2:

Building Strong Teams and Culture

CHAPTER 5:

From Porter to Principal: We All Sell Cars

Service is the thing you're doing... Hospitality is how you make people feel when you do that thing." — Will Guidara

Every individual plays a pivotal role in the operation of a dealership. From the moment a car comes out of detail and onto the lot to the time it finds its way into a customer's driveway, it's not just a transaction; it's a journey. This journey relies on a united team effort, where every role, from the porter to the dealer principal, is essential. Together, we create something greater than the sum of its parts: A culture of service, respect, and excellence.

As leaders and team members, we must understand that success in this business isn't about individual glory—it's about how well we serve others. Whether it's a customer or a colleague, true leadership comes from humility, collaboration, and the commitment to making people feel valued.

Ego Has No Place Here

Ego has no place within the four walls of a dealership. Every day, we have the opportunity to create a thriving community where each role contributes to the larger goal: Serving our customers' transportation needs. From the meticulous porter ensuring vehicles shine to the dealer principal crafting a vision for growth, every position is crucial in keeping the wheels turning.

The connection between roles isn't hierarchical—it's collaborative. When we honor one another's contributions and share knowledge freely, the dealership becomes more than a business. It becomes a family united by a shared mission. By serving one another, we amplify our strengths and minimize our weaknesses.

As F&I professionals, our role transcends the paperwork and numbers. We are the bridge between the customer's dream and reality, ensuring their experience is seamless and memorable. This requires early involvement and collaboration with the sales department. When we work together, we craft solutions that align perfectly with the customer's needs, creating not just a sale but a meaningful experience.

The Role of Servant Leadership

Servant leadership transforms a dealership from a workplace into a community. A servant leader prioritizes the growth, well-being, and success of their team, knowing this directly translates into exceptional customer experiences.

Here's a practical example: Imagine a sales associate who needs help finalizing a deal. Instead of leaving them to struggle, the F&I Manager steps in early, providing insights that not only close the sale but enhance the customer's satisfaction. That's servant leadership in action—lifting others to achieve a shared goal.

Empathy is another cornerstone of servant leadership. When we take the time to understand the emotions and motivations of both our team and our customers, we create an environment of trust and collaboration. By focusing on their needs, we naturally elevate the dealership's performance and culture.

Lessons from "Unreasonable Hospitality"

I recently read *Unreasonable Hospitality* by Will Guidara, a book that every automotive professional should read. It emphasizes the transformative power of creating memorable experiences by going beyond expectations. Guidara's success at Eleven Madison Park came from building a culture of hospitality—a way of making people feel seen, valued, and cared for. This mindset applies directly to our industry. Service is what we do, but hospitality is how we make people feel while doing it.

Do you treat your retail clients like guests in your home? This simple perspective shift can set your dealership apart. When the entire team adopts this mentality, it's not just the customers who benefit. Team members feel more connected and valued, creating an unbreakable culture of pride, collaboration, and excellence.

Real Stories of Collaboration

Throughout my career, I've witnessed countless examples of team members stepping outside their defined roles to serve the greater good. Whether it's a porter ensuring a vehicle is spotless for delivery or a sales manager helping the F&I Department during a rush, these acts of service strengthen the dealership's foundation.

F&I professionals who embrace collaboration become linchpins in the operation. By engaging with the sales team early and often, they bridge the gap between customer needs and dealership goals, ensuring that every interaction leaves a lasting positive impression.

Key Takeaways

1. **Every Role Matters:** From porter to principal, every team member plays a critical part in the dealership's success.
2. **Collaboration Is Key:** Open communication and teamwork elevate the customer experience and boost morale.
3. **Hospitality Creates Loyalty:** Treat customers like guests in your home to build trust and long-term relationships.
4. **Servant Leadership Drives Success:** Leading with humility and a focus on serving others fosters unity and operational excellence.
5. **Culture Is Everything:** A culture of respect and collaboration transforms a dealership into a thriving, unified team.

Action Steps

For F&I Professionals

1. Collaborate with the sales team early to understand customer needs.
2. Build trust with other departments to ensure seamless operations.
3. Treat every customer interaction as an opportunity to create value and connection.

For Dealership Teams

1. Host cross-departmental training sessions to foster communication and mutual respect.
2. Recognize and celebrate team members who go above and beyond their roles.

3. Embrace a culture where everyone contributes to creating exceptional customer experiences.

For Leadership

1. Model servant leadership by prioritizing the growth and well-being of your team.
2. Create opportunities for team members to step outside their roles and collaborate.
3. Foster an environment where everyone feels valued and empowered.

Reflection Questions

Personal Practice

1. Do I treat every customer and team member as though they are guests in my home?

Resilience

2. How do I handle challenges that require collaboration across departments?

Teamwork

3. How do I contribute to fostering unity among all dealership roles?

Growth

4. What steps can I take to better understand and support the roles of my colleagues?

Bridging Reflection to Action

The biggest takeaway I want you to understand is simple yet profound: We all have a critical role within the dealership, and it's essential that we all row in the same direction. Together, we're not just selling cars; we're building relationships, creating memorable experiences, and fostering a legacy of service and excellence.

When we embrace humility, collaboration, and servant leadership, we create a dealership culture that thrives. The results speak for themselves—not just in sales but in trust, loyalty, and pride. Let's move forward with a shared mission to serve, grow, and lead with integrity.

CHAPTER 6:
The Prima Donna

"True leadership is about service, not status. It's about lifting others, not elevating yourself." — Unknown

This is a topic I know intimately—I am a recovering prima donna. In my 20s, I believed the sales department revolved around me. I would complain about cash deals and grow frustrated with my desk manager over deal structures. I'd grumble about staying late and rarely stepped out of my office to help the sales team unless it directly benefited me. Does this sound familiar? I can't be the only F&I Manager guilty of this behavior.

I share this with humility and a touch of humor because I've had the honor of visiting thousands of dealerships, and let me tell you—I've seen it all. This behavior isn't unique, but it's something we must recognize and address if we want to evolve as professionals and leaders.

The Turning Point

Something shifted for me in my early 30s—a light bulb moment, an "aha!" realization. I finally understood that treating my sales team with respect, collaborating with my desk manager, and investing in human capital wasn't just the right thing to do—it was the most profitable approach.

Fast forward to today: I now run multiple successful companies fueled by teams that serve one another. It's a beautiful sight as a business owner to witness collaboration, planning, and execution at the highest levels. This didn't happen by accident—it required intentional change, a shift from self-centeredness to servant leadership.

The Origin of the Prima Donna Archetype

The term prima donna, derived from the Italian phrase meaning 'first lady,' originated in opera during the 18th century. It described the lead female singer known for her exceptional talent and commanding stage presence. Over time, the term evolved to characterize individuals—regardless of gender—who demand special treatment and exhibit entitlement.

In the context of a dealership, a prima donna often manifests as someone with undeniable talent but an attitude that disrupts teamwork and undermines the organization's culture.

Characteristics of a Prima Donna

1. **Exceptional Talent:** Their skills are undeniable, but their self-image often inflates, leading them to believe they deserve special treatment.
2. **Demanding Nature:** Prima donnas set high expectations for others but rarely hold themselves to the same standard.
3. **Attention-Seeking Behavior:** They crave validation and often overshadow their colleagues' efforts.
4. **Emotional Volatility:** Quick to react defensively to criticism, prima donnas often create tension within teams.
5. **Resistance to Teamwork:** They view collaboration as optional and prioritize personal success over collective goals.

Sound familiar? If so, don't worry—change is possible.

Shifting from Prima Donna to Servant Leader

Becoming a servant leader means replacing entitlement with humility, selfishness with service, and isolation with collaboration. It's about recognizing that leadership is not about being the center of attention but about lifting others to achieve shared success.

Let me tell you what happens when you shed Prima Donna tendencies: You build trust. You create harmony within your team. You foster an environment where collaboration flourishes and everyone thrives. Most importantly, you become a leader who serves, inspires, and drives meaningful results.

A Personal Example: The Ripple Effect of Change

I'll never forget the transformation I witnessed in one dealership. The top-performing F&I Manager was a textbook prima donna—brilliant but divisive. After a candid conversation, he embraced change and started getting out of his office and out on the showroom floor early and often. By doing these things, he earned respect from his sales associates and sales managers that led to improved relationships, a stronger team dynamic, and record-breaking months for the dealership. When you trade ego for empathy, amazing things happen.

How Prima Donna Behaviors Impact Customers

Prima donna tendencies don't just affect internal relationships—they trickle down to the customer experience. When an F&I Manager prioritizes their convenience over collaboration, it creates friction that customers can sense. On the flip side, a culture of servant leadership ensures that every customer feels valued and understood.

Strategies for Overcoming Prima Donna Tendencies

If you recognize yourself in this chapter, take heart—awareness is the first step toward growth. Here's how to start:

1. **Practice Humility:** Acknowledge the contributions of others and express gratitude regularly.
2. **Embrace Collaboration:** View teamwork as a strength, not a burden. Offer to help colleagues without expecting something in return.
3. **Seek Feedback:** Ask your team how you can improve. Be open to constructive criticism.
4. **Prioritize Service:** Make serving your team and customers your top priority.
5. **Commit to Growth:** Invest in personal and professional development to stay aligned with servant leadership principles.

Summary

The prima donna archetype, while often celebrated for talent, can create disruption and division. By recognizing and addressing these behaviors, we can shift from entitlement to empowerment, building stronger teams and creating exceptional customer experiences. Servant leadership transforms prima donnas into collaborative, empathetic leaders who inspire and uplift everyone around them.

Key Takeaways

1. **Humility Is Strength:** Leadership is about service, not self-importance.
2. **Collaboration Drives Success:** Strong teams outperform isolated individuals.
3. **Empathy Enhances Relationships:** Understanding others' perspectives fosters trust and respect.
4. **Customer Focus Wins:** A culture of service elevates the customer experience.
5. **Growth Is Essential:** Continuous self-awareness and improvement are the foundations of servant leadership.

Action Steps

For F&I Managers

1. Shadow a sales associate for a day to gain perspective.
2. Schedule regular check-ins with your sales team to build rapport.
3. Practice gratitude by publicly acknowledging team contributions.

For Dealership Teams

1. Create team-building activities to foster collaboration.
2. Host a workshop on servant leadership principles.
3. Develop a feedback system to encourage honest communication.

For Individual Professionals

1. Reflect on your behaviors—are they helping or hindering your team?
2. Dedicate time to learning about servant leadership.
3. Seek mentorship from leaders who exemplify humility and service.

How to Apply This

In the F&I Office

Start each day by asking, "How can I serve my team and customers better today?" Make collaboration with the sales department a non-negotiable part of your routine.

Across the Dealership

Promote a culture of mutual respect by aligning all departments with a shared mission. Encourage open communication and recognize team wins.

In Your Daily Practice

Commit to self-awareness. Regularly assess your actions and their impact on others and strive to replace prima donna behaviors with servant leadership values.

Practical Tools for Success

1. **Reflection Prompts:**
   i.   "Am I fostering collaboration or creating friction?"
   ii. "How do my actions impact my team and customers?"
2. **Team Feedback System:** Develop a system for anonymous feedback to identify areas for growth.
3. **Mentorship Opportunities:** Pair prima donnas with servant leaders to model collaborative behavior.

Bridging Reflection to Action

Reflecting on the prima donna archetype, consider the ways in which ego may be limiting your potential. By embracing servant leadership, you unlock the ability to inspire, uplift, and drive meaningful change.

In the next chapter, we'll explore how mentorship can transform not only individuals but entire organizations. Let's step into the next phase of your journey and learn how to guide others toward greatness.

CHAPTER 7:

The Sales Manager Is the F&I Manager's Best Friend

"Success in any dealership is the result of collaboration, not competition, between the finance manager and sales manager." — Adam Marburger

When I entered the automotive industry in 1999, I immediately noticed tension between the sales and F&I departments. It often felt as though they were working against each other rather than as a cohesive team. Over the years, I've learned that a strong relationship between the sales manager and the F&I Manager is not only essential but also transformational.

This chapter explores the dynamic and sometimes complicated relationship between these two key roles and offers strategies for fostering collaboration to drive profitability, customer satisfaction, and dealership success.

Early Lessons in Teamwork

During my first dealership role, I saw firsthand how animosity between the sales and F&I teams could hurt morale and performance. This division often stemmed from a lack of communication, conflicting goals, and unresolved frustrations. When I moved to a new dealership and earned the role of F&I Manager, I quickly realized that success was impossible without bridging this gap.

One pivotal moment came on a chaotic Saturday when a fiery F&I Manager quit on the spot. It was my chance to step up, and though I was green, I knew I needed to prove that collaboration—not conflict—was the way forward. Looking back, that experience set the foundation for my commitment to fostering teamwork and mutual respect between F&I and sales teams.

Understanding Roles and Responsibilities

The Finance Manager

The F&I Manager's role is multifaceted, encompassing deal structuring, compliance, and maximizing profitability through product offerings. These professionals are the dealership's financial architects, ensuring that deals align with customer needs while supporting the dealership's bottom line.

The Sales Manager

The sales manager is the leader of the showroom floor and is responsible for driving volume, maintaining customer relationships, and managing the sales team. Their success hinges on effective communication, strong leadership, and the ability to close deals efficiently.

Building Bridges: Collaboration in Action

Shared Goals for Mutual Success

While the F&I and sales teams have distinct responsibilities, their ultimate goal is the same: To sell vehicles and maximize profitability. By aligning their objectives and working together, they can create a seamless transaction process that enhances both customer satisfaction and dealership revenue.

Communication Is Key

Regular communication is the cornerstone of a strong F&I-sales partnership. Weekly strategy meetings, daily check-ins, and shared problem-solving sessions help keep both managers aligned. When sales teams understand F&I products, they can better position them during the transaction, increasing conversion rates.

Case Studies: Success Stories

Case Study 1: The Power of Collaboration

In a mid-sized dealership, the finance and sales managers initiated weekly strategy meetings. By discussing current promotions, incentives, and financing options, they created a shared vision for success. This collaboration led to enhanced communication and, ultimately, increased sales and profitability.

Case Study 2: Navigating Challenges

Another dealership faced tension when the sales manager frequently offered buy rates on the first pencil, which the finance manager found unsustainable. By implementing a structured and compliant approach, they agreed to set limits on rate discounts. This compromise ensured profitability while still providing competitive rates to customers. The result? Increased F&I revenue with satisfied customers.

Case Study 3: The Bash Brothers

At one dealership, the sales manager and F&I Manager worked side-by-side at the desk, operating as a single unit. Their shared goal was simple: Sell vehicles while maximizing gross profit. By combining their strengths, they achieved unprecedented results, enhancing profitability and delivering a seamless customer experience.

This final case study is the story of Pete and me—a partnership that exemplifies the power of collaboration.

The Story of Adam and Pete: The Bash Brothers

Pete and I didn't hit it off at first. We were close in age and experience and often butted heads over everything, from deal structures to customer interactions. But one day, we decided to set our egos aside and forge a pact: We would work as one unit to maximize both front-end and back-end gross profits.

Pete hated taking customer T/Os (turnovers), so I stepped in to handle them. This allowed me to control transactions early and avoid unnecessary complications. Over time, our partnership transformed into a powerhouse of collaboration. Pete's deep understanding of lending guidelines, paired with my customer-facing skills, created an unbeatable dynamic.

We dubbed ourselves "The Bash Brothers," after the Oakland A's stars Jose Canseco and Mark McGwire. Together, we became known for delivering high gross profits, nearly flawless CITs, and impeccable CSI scores. Our partnership not only enhanced dealership success but also turned us into lifelong friends.

The Cornerstone of Dealership Success

The relationship between the finance manager and sales manager is a cornerstone of success in an automotive dealership. By fostering collaboration, maintaining open lines of communication, and addressing challenges proactively, these two key players can create a harmonious and productive environment.

The result is not just increased sales and profitability but also a better experience for customers, who benefit from a seamless purchasing process. As the automotive industry continues to evolve, the partnership between finance and sales will remain critical in navigating the complexities of today's marketplace.

My recommendation is to invest in this relationship, as it will pay massive dividends. Building mutual respect, fostering collaboration, and aligning shared goals will ensure not only operational success but also long-term growth and loyalty from both customers and team members.

Summary

The relationship between the sales manager and the F&I Manager is foundational to dealership success. By fostering collaboration, maintaining open communication, and addressing challenges proactively, these two roles can create a powerhouse partnership. This not only increases sales and profitability but also enhances the customer experience. As the automotive industry continues to evolve, investing in this relationship will yield long-term dividends.

Key Takeaways

1. **Shared Goals Lead to Success**: Align F&I and sales objectives for mutual benefit.
2. **Communication Is Non-Negotiable**: Regular, transparent communication builds trust and efficiency.
3. **Conflict Is Inevitable—Resolve It**: Address disagreements with openness and a focus on shared outcomes.
4. **Training Builds Understanding**: Cross-training fosters respect and collaboration.
5. **Self-Awareness Is Crucial**: Reflect on your role and how it supports the sales team's success.

Action Steps

For F&I Managers

1. Schedule weekly meetings with the sales manager to align goals.
2. Spend time shadowing sales activities to gain perspective.
3. Proactively engage in deal structuring early in the process.

For Sales Managers

1. Learn the basics of F&I product offerings to better position them.
2. Encourage your team to set up F&I for success by creating warm hand-offs.
3. Work collaboratively with F&I to maximize profitability.

For Dealership Teams

1. Implement cross-department training sessions.
2. Foster a culture of open communication and mutual respect.
3. Celebrate shared successes to reinforce collaboration.

Reflection Questions

Personal Practice

1. Am I fostering collaboration or creating friction between sales and F&I?
2. How can I better align my actions with the dealership's shared goals?

Resilience

1. How do I navigate conflicts between sales and F&I effectively?
2. What steps can I take to build trust with my counterpart?

Growth

1. How can I develop skills that enhance my ability to collaborate across departments?
2. What opportunities exist for cross-training in my dealership?

Bridging Reflection to Action

As you reflect on the importance of collaboration, consider how you can take proactive steps to strengthen your relationship with your counterpart. Whether it's scheduling a meeting, addressing lingering conflicts, or simply offering a helping hand, these small actions will pave the way for greater success.

CHAPTER 8:
Processes Do Not Fail, People Fail Processes

"Efficiency is doing things right; effectiveness is doing the right things."
— Peter Drucker

In the sometimes-hectic world of automotive dealerships, the myriad of distractions and constant movement can often create an environment ripe for chaos. Phones are ringing, deals are being structured, service bays are buzzing, and every department feels like a whirlwind of activity. Yet amidst this chaos, one fundamental truth remains: **Processes do not fail; people fail processes.**

For those aspiring to achieve excellence in their roles, especially in F&I, embracing well-defined processes is non-negotiable. While discussing processes may not be the most glamorous topic, I can tell you from visiting thousands of dealerships nationwide: **Those who follow defined processes consistently outperform their peers.**

The Foundation of Success

At the heart of every successful dealership is a robust framework of processes. These processes act as the operational backbone, ensuring efficiency, consistency, and accountability. However, a process is only as effective as the people executing it.

Top achievers understand that success isn't just about talent or hard work—it's about executing a system with precision. When everyone adheres to the same playbook, it reduces errors, miscommunication, and inefficiencies while driving team cohesion and better outcomes.

The Distractions of the Dealership

Distractions are abundant in a dealership environment. Sales consultants might get lost in CRM updates or customer negotiations. F&I professionals are pulled between processing deals, cleaning CITs, and answering calls from lenders to rehash approvals. These distractions can derail even the best-intentioned teams.

Without adherence to a defined process, the chaos can compromise customer satisfaction, profitability, and even team morale. For instance, skipping steps in an F&I transaction can result in missed opportunities, lost revenue, and dissatisfied customers. The reality is: **The process is not the problem—it's the lack of adherence to it.**

I've seen this firsthand. Dealerships that run like well-oiled machines are not just "lucky." They're disciplined. Processes create a framework for consistency, allowing teams to focus on what matters most—serving the customer.

The Role of Leadership

Great leaders understand the importance of instilling respect for processes within their teams. This isn't about micromanaging; it's about creating an environment where the process becomes the standard.

As a leader:

1. **Lead by Example:** Your actions set the tone. Follow the processes yourself, demonstrating their importance.
2. **Train and Reinforce:** Regular training ensures everyone understands their role and contribution to the process.
3. **Recognize and Reward:** Celebrate team members who consistently follow the process. Recognition reinforces adherence and motivates others.

Servant leaders prioritize the development of their teams by ensuring everyone is equipped with the tools, training, and mindset to succeed. This commitment to empowering others elevates the entire dealership.

Growth and Profitability Through Process

When processes are followed, dealerships experience:

1. **Improved Efficiency:** Consistent workflows reduce wasted time and eliminate guesswork.

2. **Higher Profitability:** Adherence ensures upsell opportunities, minimized mistakes, and better inventory management.
3. **Enhanced Customer Satisfaction:** A seamless, professional experience fosters loyalty and referrals.

Take a moment to reflect

1. Do you have a written, defined process for your F&I operations?
2. Do you follow it on every transaction?
3. Is someone in your dealership holding everyone accountable to the process?

If you answered "yes," congratulations—you're ahead of the curve. If not, start today. Processes are the foundation of excellence, and it's never too late to refine and commit to them.

F&I Black Belt Road to Sale

To maximize F&I profitability while enhancing the customer experience, I've developed a nine-step process. This approach ensures consistency and effectiveness in every transaction. Follow these steps, and you'll be on the path to becoming an F&I Black Belt:

1. **Early F&I Touch:** If possible, introduce yourself to the retail customer before they agree to purchase. The idea is to show professionalism and make a great first impression. This will pay off later during your menu presentation and objection handling.
2. **Deal Audit:** Make sure the deal is clean and ready for F&I to process. Hold all parties accountable for incomplete or inaccurate documentation. Slow down, take notes, and use a deal checklist on every transaction.
3. **Sales Manager Conversation:** When possible, attempt to work the deal with your sales manager. Offer to get involved early in the transaction. The earlier F&I gets involved, the higher the gross profit. Always make yourself available to your desk and sales staff.
4. **Sales Consultant Conversation:** Get as much information about your client and their buying motives from the sales consultant. Identify the decision-maker's personality type. Always thank your sales consultant for the opportunity and look for ways to mentor your team.
5. **Customer Conversation:** Congratulate your customers and thank them for their business. Build rapport by serving them and

developing a genuine relationship. If the customer likes you, they're more likely to buy from you.

6. **Factory Warranty Presentation:** Explain what is covered and not covered by the manufacturer's warranty. Break down your dealership's parts and labor rates. Do not attempt to sell during this step—simply inform.

7. **Menu Presentation:** Every product, every customer, every time. Present a menu to everyone without exceptions. You should genuinely believe in every product you offer.

8. **Close and Disclose:** Help your client select appropriate coverage and disclose all pricing. This is the fun part—if you've followed the process, this step becomes a natural conclusion.

9. **Ensure Customer Satisfaction:** Your goal isn't just to sell a car today—it's to build relationships for tomorrow. The F&I office leaves a lasting impression on your customers; make it a positive one.

Summary

Processes don't fail—people do. Success lies in defining clear, actionable steps and committing to following them consistently. Exceptional leaders instill respect for these processes, fostering a culture of accountability and teamwork.

When you and your team embrace process adherence, distractions are minimized, customer satisfaction improves, and profitability soars. Commit to mastering your processes and watch as your dealership transforms into a model of excellence.

Key Takeaways

1. **Processes Are the Backbone:** They ensure consistency and efficiency in operations.

2. **Leadership Sets the Tone:** Leaders must model process adherence and reinforce its importance.

3. **Processes Drive Profitability:** Defined workflows enhance customer satisfaction and financial outcomes.

4. **F&I Black Belt Process Works:** Following a structured approach ensures success for both the dealership and the customer.

5. **Commitment Is Key:** Consistency in following processes separates top achievers from the rest.

Action Steps

For F&I Managers

1. Commit to the F&I Black Belt Road to Sale process.
2. Review your daily workflow and identify areas for improvement.

For Dealership Teams

1. Hold regular training sessions on process adherence.
2. Celebrate team members who excel in following defined workflows.

For Individual Professionals

1. Reflect on your personal adherence to processes.
2. Seek mentorship or training to refine your approach.

Reflection Questions

1. Am I following the defined processes consistently?
2. How can I encourage my team to prioritize process adherence?
3. What adjustments can I make to minimize distractions?

By adhering to well-defined processes, you can transform your dealership into a powerhouse of efficiency, profitability, and customer satisfaction. In the next chapter, we'll explore the importance of collaboration across departments and how to foster a culture of mutual success. Stay tuned for more actionable insights!

Bridging Reflection to Action

Processes are the backbone of any successful dealership, but their true power is only realized when people commit to executing them with precision. Reflect on your own adherence to defined workflows: Are you consistent, or do distractions sometimes pull you off track? By embracing discipline and accountability, you can transform processes into tools for efficiency, profitability, and customer satisfaction.

In the next chapter, we'll explore the symbiotic relationship between Service and F&I, revealing how collaboration between these departments can drive loyalty, retention, and long-term success.

SECTION 3:

Mastering the F&I Craft

CHAPTER 9:

The Symbiotic Relationship Between Service and F&I

"Customers may forget what you said, but they'll never forget how you made them feel." — Maya Angelou

The goal of a thriving F&I department is simple yet impactful: To get the retail customer happily engaged with the service department. A satisfied service customer is far more likely to return for their next vehicle purchase, creating a cycle of loyalty and profitability. To achieve this, dealerships must offer retention-based products that bond customers to the service department, creating a seamless bridge between the initial sale and ongoing engagement.

The relationship between service and F&I isn't just about operational alignment—it's symbiotic. Each department amplifies the other, fostering customer satisfaction, enhancing dealership retention, and driving revenue.

Understanding the Value of Service Loyalty

Statistical evidence consistently highlights that customers who utilize the dealership's service department are more likely to return for future purchases. This loyalty stems from the trust and familiarity cultivated through regular service visits. When customers interact with the same service advisors and experience consistently excellent care, they begin to view the dealership as a partner in their automotive journey.

Servicing vehicles at the dealership also provides tangible benefits, such as manufacturer-approved parts and trained technicians. This not only ensures peak vehicle performance but also safeguards resale value. These factors create a compelling reason for customers to stay loyal to the dealership.

The Role of F&I Products in Retention

F&I products serve as the bridge between sales and service. When presented effectively, they address customer concerns and add value to their ownership experience. Products like vehicle service agreements (VSCs), maintenance plans, and appearance protection directly tie customers to the dealership's service department, reinforcing loyalty while alleviating the financial stress of unexpected repairs.

Practical Tip

F&I Managers should dedicate time to mastering their product knowledge. The more confident and knowledgeable you are, the more effectively you can communicate the value of these offerings.

Creating a Collaborative Environment

A robust relationship between the service and F&I departments requires open communication and shared goals.

1. Training and Alignment:
   i. Hold regular meetings to ensure service advisors understand the value of F&I products.
   ii. Service advisors don't need to sell these products, but they should understand how to identify opportunities, and pass leads to F&I Managers.
2. Building Mutual Understanding:
   i. F&I Managers should spend time with service advisors to understand their workflows.
   ii. Service advisors should shadow F&I Managers to gain insight into product offerings and customer benefits.

Example

When service advisors notice aging vehicles or customers expressing repair concerns, they can introduce relevant F&I products as solutions, creating a smoother transition for future vehicle purchases.

Leveraging Technology for Enhanced Engagement

In the digital age, technology is essential for maintaining and strengthening the service-F&I connection.

1. **CRM Integration:** Track service history, customer preferences, and F&I product uptake to personalize interactions.
2. **Automated Follow-Ups:** Send reminders for service appointments and tailored offers for Vehicles Service Contracts or maintenance plans.

Pro Tip

Post-sale F&I opportunities in the service drive are often underutilized. Implementing these processes ensures customers receive value while boosting gross profits.

Summary: A Symbiotic Relationship

The partnership between the service and F&I departments is a win-win for dealerships and customers. Service departments build trust through care and expertise, while F&I enhances the ownership experience with valuable products. When these teams align with a shared vision of customer satisfaction, they create a powerful cycle of loyalty and profitability.

Key Takeaways:

1. **Customer Retention Is Key:** Loyal service customers are more likely to return for future purchases.
2. **F&I Products Drive Engagement:** Properly presented F&I products tie customers to the service department.
3. **Collaboration Enhances Outcomes:** Open communication between service and F&I ensures seamless customer experiences.
4. **Technology Is a Game-Changer:** CRM tools and automated follow-ups maintain customer connections.
5. **Continuous Improvement Matters:** Regular training and alignment strengthen interdepartmental relationships.

Action Steps

For F&I Managers

1. Spend time in the service department to understand its workflows and customer interactions.
2. Schedule training sessions with service advisors to discuss the value of F&I products.

For Dealership Teams

1. Host monthly cross-department meetings to align goals and strategies.
2. Use CRM data to identify opportunities for follow-ups and personalized offers.

For Individual Professionals

1. Reflect on how your role supports the dealership's retention goals.
2. Continuously improve your product knowledge to communicate value effectively.

How to Apply This

In the F&I Office

1. Proactively collaborate with service advisors to identify customer needs.
2. Use data to personalize product presentations that emphasize service-related benefits.

Across the Dealership

1. Encourage a culture of teamwork between Service and F&I.
2. Recognize and reward efforts that enhance cross-departmental collaboration.

In Your Daily Practice

1. Dedicate time to understanding how your actions impact customer retention.
2. Seek feedback from service advisors to refine your approach.

Practical Tools for Success

1. **Service-F&I Collaboration Playbook:** A guide for aligning goals and processes between departments.
2. **CRM Dashboard:** Track service history, F&I product uptake, and customer preferences.
3. **Training Modules:** Focused on helping service advisors understand and recommend F&I products.

Reflection Questions

Personal Practice

1. How often do I engage with the service department to identify opportunities?

Resilience

2. What challenges have I faced in aligning with the service team, and how did I overcome them?

Teamwork

3. What can I do to improve collaboration between service and F&I?

Growth

4. How can I better utilize technology to enhance customer retention?

Bridging Reflection to Action:

Take a moment to evaluate the relationship between your service and F&I departments. Identify one actionable step you can take today to enhance collaboration and customer retention. In the next chapter, we'll explore the pivotal role of processes in ensuring dealership success.

CHAPTER 10:

The Earlier F&I is Involved, the More Profitable the Transaction

"The deal isn't a deal until the F&I department makes it a deal. Get them involved early, and you'll turn good deals into great ones."
— Adam Marburger

In the fast-paced environment of automotive dealerships, timing can mean the difference between profitability and mediocrity. One of the most overlooked strategies for maximizing gross profit and customer satisfaction is involving the F&I department early in the sales process. The F&I team, often viewed as the dealership's closers, holds the expertise, insight, and persuasive communication skills needed to elevate the customer experience while maximizing gross profit.

The Value of F&I Early Involvement

F&I professionals are more than just the last step in the sales process—they are integral to the entire transaction. When engaged early, they can:

1. Identify potential challenges in deal structures.
2. Offer tailored financial solutions that resonate with the customer's needs.
3. Help the sales team navigate complex financing scenarios.
4. Lay the groundwork for smoother closings.

By empowering the F&I department to interact directly with customers during the early stages of the buying journey, dealerships can maximize the use of their talent and expertise.

Integrating F&I into the Sales Process

A practical rule in my dealership was simple but powerful: If F&I Managers weren't actively working on a deal, they needed to be on the showroom floor or sitting at the sales desk. This practice ensured seamless collaboration between sales and F&I, ultimately creating a unified front for serving the customer.

F&I professionals should:

1. **Engage Early**: Meet customers during their initial interactions with the dealership to establish rapport.
2. **Collaborate with Sales Managers**: Work together to structure deals that maximize profitability and ensure customer satisfaction.
3. **Identify Opportunities**: Assess customer profiles to determine the best financing and F&I product options.

By aligning these strategies, the dealership not only improves gross profitability but also enhances the overall customer experience.

The Superpowers of the F&I Department

The F&I department's "superpowers" lie in their ability to:

1. **Create Tailored Solutions**: Address individual financial needs with precision.
2. **Navigate Complexity**: Resolve challenging financing situations with confidence.
3. **Build Trust**: Foster rapport with customers to ease the transaction process.
4. **Enhance Decision-Making**: Identify personality types and past purchasing behaviors to customize their approach.

These strengths, when leveraged early, ensure a streamlined process, reduce customer apprehension, and maximize product penetrations.

Summary

Involving the F&I department early in the transaction leads to:

1. Increased gross profit per vehicle.
2. Higher acceptance rates of F&I products.
3. Improved customer satisfaction and retention.
4. A collaborative culture between sales and F&I teams.

The earlier F&I Managers engage with customers, the more they can tailor the experience to meet customer needs and financial goals, ultimately enhancing profitability and dealership culture.

Key Takeaways

1. The deal isn't complete until F&I professionals make it so.
2. Early F&I involvement prevents last-minute deal roadblocks.
3. F&I and sales collaboration fosters a seamless customer experience.
4. Empowering F&I professionals leads to higher gross profit and retention rates.
5. Early F&I touchpoints build trust and enhance product uptake.

Action Steps

For F&I Managers

1. Step out of the office and engage with customers during their initial visits.
2. Partner with sales managers early to structure deals that work for both the dealership and the customer.
3. Continuously train to enhance your ability to identify customer needs and personality types.

For Dealership Teams

1. Encourage collaboration between sales and F&I departments.
2. Provide F&I professionals with the tools and authority to engage customers early in the process.
3. Reinforce the importance of F&I in enhancing the customer journey.

For Individual Professionals

1. Build rapport with customers by introducing yourself during the sales process.
2. Share insights and strategies with sales teams to improve deal outcomes.
3. Prioritize communication and transparency to foster trust and loyalty.

How to Apply This

In the F&I Office

1. Create a schedule that allows F&I Managers to be present on the showroom floor during downtime.
2. Use CRM tools to track customer interactions and identify opportunities for early engagement.

Across the Dealership

1. Implement policies that encourage joint meetings between sales and F&I teams.
2. Celebrate successes that stem from collaborative efforts between departments.

In Your Daily Practice

1. Approach every customer interaction with a mindset of collaboration and service.
2. Use early interactions to gather insights about customer needs, preferences, and concerns.

Practical Tools for Success

1. **Customer Profiles**: Develop a system to document customer needs, past experiences, and potential objections during early interactions.
2. **Collaboration Frameworks**: Create guidelines for how sales and F&I teams will communicate and cooperate on deals.
3. **Training Modules**: Invest in regular training to enhance F&I professionals' ability to engage customers effectively.

Bridging Reflection to Action

The early involvement of F&I professionals is not just a strategy; it's a shift in mindset. By integrating F&I into the sales process, dealerships unlock untapped potential for profitability and customer loyalty. In the next chapter, we'll explore how a commitment to ongoing training and professional development amplifies the impact of every team member, driving sustained success for the dealership.

CHAPTER 11:
Service vs. Hospitality

"Service is about what you do for people; hospitality is about how you make them feel while you're doing it."
— Danny Meyer

The distinction between service and hospitality is crucial yet often overlooked in the automotive industry. Service encompasses the actions taken—selling a car, repairing a vehicle, or processing financing applications. Hospitality, however, is about creating an emotional connection with customers, ensuring they feel valued, respected, and cared for throughout their journey with your dealership.

This chapter explores how integrating hospitality into the service framework elevates the customer experience and builds lasting relationships, creating a thriving culture for both customers and staff.

The Concept of Service

Service has long been the foundation of the automotive dealership's operations. It is defined by:

1. **Efficiency:** Timely completion of tasks.
2. **Expertise:** Offering accurate solutions and sound advice.
3. **Consistency:** Ensuring a reliable experience for every customer.

While these elements are vital, they can make the customer experience feel transactional if not accompanied by emotional connection.

The Essence of Hospitality

Hospitality goes beyond providing excellent service. It is about:

1. **Warmth:** Greeting customers with genuine friendliness.
2. **Empathy:** Understanding and responding to their unique needs.

3. **Personalization:** Tailoring every interaction to the individual.

Incorporating hospitality transforms stressful experiences—like purchasing a car or handling repairs—into opportunities to delight and engage customers.

Bridging Service and Hospitality

Treating Customers Like Guests

Imagine inviting someone into your home. You would likely ensure they feel welcome, comfortable, and cared for. This mindset should extend to dealership operations:

1. **Active Listening:** Understand customer concerns and preferences.
2. **Comfortable Environments:** Create inviting spaces for discussions.
3. **Follow-Up Care:** Ensure post-sale engagement, addressing questions or needs.

Supporting Sales Associates

Hospitality doesn't stop with customers. Creating a culture of appreciation and collaboration among staff fosters teamwork and enhances the overall dealership environment.

1. **Recognition:** Acknowledge the contributions of your sales team.
2. **Open Dialogue:** Encourage feedback to improve processes.
3. **Team-Building Activities:** Strengthen relationships among employees.

The Investment in Hospitality

Hospitality is not just a feel-good initiative—it's a strategic differentiator. Customers who feel valued are more likely to become repeat buyers and recommend your dealership to others.

Training and Development

Dealerships should invest in training programs to instill a hospitality mindset. Focus areas include:

1. Communication techniques.
2. Managing customer emotions.
3. Creating exceptional experiences.

Feedback Mechanisms

Continual improvement relies on understanding what works and what doesn't. Use tools like:

1. Customer satisfaction surveys.
2. Mystery shopper programs.
3. Regular staff discussions about experiences and insights.

Measuring Success

Evaluate the impact of hospitality initiatives through:

1. Increased retention rates.
2. Growth in referral business.
3. Higher employee satisfaction scores.

Summary

Service is about getting the job done; hospitality is about creating meaningful connections. By combining the two, F&I professionals can build trust, foster loyalty, and elevate the dealership experience for both customers and employees.

Key Takeaways

1. Service is transactional; hospitality is emotional.
2. Treat every customer like a guest in your home.
3. Hospitality strengthens relationships and builds loyalty.
4. A culture of collaboration enhances both staff and customer satisfaction.
5. Investing in hospitality yields long-term benefits in retention and referrals.

Action Steps

For F&I Managers:

1. Integrate hospitality into your customer interactions.
2. Educate yourself on emotional intelligence to better connect with clients.
3. Actively support and collaborate with sales associates.

For Dealership Teams

1. Host cross-departmental training on service and hospitality integration.
2. Share positive customer feedback to motivate and inspire the team.
3. Organize team-building activities to promote unity.

For Individual Professionals

1. Make it a habit to greet customers warmly and genuinely.
2. Regularly seek feedback to improve your approach.
3. Celebrate small wins in customer satisfaction as personal victories.

How to Apply This

In the F&I Office

Create a welcoming environment by focusing on building rapport during conversations and ensuring customers feel respected and understood.

Across the Dealership

Align all departments with a shared goal of combining service and hospitality, ensuring a consistent experience for every customer.

In Your Daily Practice

Take time to reflect on how each interaction can exceed customer expectations.

Practical Tools for Success

1. Self-Reflection Prompts:
    i. Did I make my customer feel valued today?
    ii. How can I improve my next interaction?
2. Checklist for Hospitality Excellence:
    i. Was the customer greeted warmly?
    ii. Were their concerns addressed thoughtfully?
    iii. Did I follow up after the sale?
3. Role-Playing Scenarios:
    i. Practice handling customer objections with empathy and understanding.
    ii. Simulate conversations that focus on personalization.

Bridging Reflection to Action

Service ensures tasks are completed; hospitality ensures they are remembered. The next chapter will delve into the critical role of trust in building customer relationships and how it serves as the foundation for dealership success.

By merging service and hospitality, you'll not only meet customer expectations but exceed them—transforming your dealership into a hub of excellence and trust.

CHAPTER 12:
The Art of Persuasion

"True persuasion lies in empowering others to make the best decisions for themselves, guided by empathy and trust." – Unknown

The ability to persuade is not merely a skill—it's an art form that goes hand in hand with leadership. For F&I Managers striving to embody servant leadership, mastering the art of persuasion is essential. Persuasion, when used with integrity, becomes a tool to help others make informed decisions that align with their needs and values. This chapter will guide you through understanding and applying the principles of persuasion, leveraging personality types, and adopting a customer-first mindset that fosters trust and collaboration.

The Foundation of Persuasion

At its core, persuasion is about influence—not manipulation. It's about connecting with customers on a personal level and helping them make decisions that align with their goals. Effective persuasion begins with:

1. **Active Listening**: Paying attention to what customers are saying—and what they're not saying.
2. **Empathy**: Understanding their concerns and addressing their priorities.
3. **Flexibility**: Adapting your approach to their personality and communication style.

Moving Beyond Scripted Dialogues

Traditional scripts and word tracks can be limiting, robotic, and impersonal. Customers today value authenticity and connection. Instead of relying on scripts, focus on creating genuine, tailored interactions. This involves:

1. Asking **open-ended questions** to encourage dialogue.
2. Observing **body language and emotional cues** to guide conversations.
3. Adapting your language to match their tone and style.

By moving beyond scripts, you can create trust-filled interactions that resonate.

Understanding Personality Types and Cialdini's Principles of Persuasion

Dr. Robert Cialdini's six principles of persuasion provide a roadmap for understanding customer behavior and tailoring your approach. Here's how these principles can be applied:

1. Reciprocity

When you offer something of value, customers feel obligated to reciprocate. Examples include:

1. Providing complimentary services, like a car wash or inspection.
2. Sharing free educational resources about F&I products.
3. Sending thank-you notes or small post-sale gifts to foster goodwill.

2. Commitment and Consistency

Once customers make a small commitment, they're more likely to follow through on larger ones. Examples include:

1. Asking them to agree to a small benefit, like a complimentary warranty.
2. Reinforcing their values, like safety, through product recommendations.

3. Social Proof

People look to others for guidance. Examples include:

1. Highlighting customer testimonials or reviews.
2. Sharing data, such as "80% of our customers choose this service plan."

4. Authority

People trust experts. Examples include:

1. Displaying certifications and achievements.

2. Positioning yourself as a consultant, not just a salesperson.

5. Liking

We are more likely to buy from those we like. Build rapport by:

1. Finding common ground and shared interests.
2. Offering genuine compliments about their decisions.

6. Scarcity

Limited availability enhances desirability. Examples include:

1. Offering limited-time promotions.
2. Emphasizing the exclusivity of certain products.

Applying the Art of Persuasion in the F&I Office

Understanding personality types helps tailor your approach:

1. **Analytical Customers**: Focus on data, logic, and detailed explanations.
2. **Expressive Customers**: Use emotion and storytelling to connect.
3. **Driver Customers**: Be direct and focus on results.
4. **Amiable Customers**: Build trust and emphasize relationships.

Embracing Servant Leadership in Persuasion

Servant leadership transforms persuasion from selling to serving. It involves:

1. **Empowering Customers**: Educate them, encourage questions, and respect their decisions.
2. **Building Trust**: Be transparent, maintain integrity, and focus on long-term relationships.

Summary

The art of persuasion isn't about convincing customers—it's about connecting with them. By understanding their needs, tailoring your approach, and applying Cialdini's principles with empathy, you can build trust and create value. As a servant leader, your goal is to empower customers to make decisions they feel good about, fostering loyalty and satisfaction.

Key Takeaways

1. Persuasion is about empowering, not pressuring, customers.
2. Personalization builds trust—move beyond scripts.
3. Understanding personality types allows for tailored approaches.
4. Cialdini's principles (reciprocity, authority, social proof, etc.) provide a framework for effective persuasion.
5. Servant leadership transforms persuasion into a tool for trust and collaboration.

Action Steps

For F&I Managers

1. Practice active listening to better understand customer needs.
2. Use open-ended questions to encourage dialogue.
3. Apply Cialdini's principles in daily interactions.

For Dealership Teams

1. Train team members on personalized persuasion techniques.
2. Share customer testimonials and success stories to reinforce social proof.

For Individual Professionals

1. Reflect on past customer interactions and identify areas for improvement.
2. Focus on building rapport and finding common ground with customers.

How to Apply This

In the F&I Office

1. Offer small acts of goodwill to create reciprocity.
2. Position yourself as an expert to build authority.

Across the Dealership

1. Promote a culture of trust by encouraging authentic, customer-first interactions.
2. Use team meetings to share persuasion success stories and strategies.

In Your Daily Practice

1. Reflect on each interaction to identify ways to build stronger connections.
2. Focus on developing empathy and flexibility in your communication.

Practical Tools for Success

1. **Customer Personality Checklist**: A quick guide to identifying personality types.
2. **Cialdini Principles Worksheet**: Practice applying the six principles in real scenarios.
3. **Reflection Journal**: Track and analyze daily interactions to refine your persuasion techniques.

Reflection Questions

Personal Practice

1. How can I adapt my communication style to connect with different personality types?

Resilience

2. How do I maintain authenticity and empathy during challenging interactions?

Teamwork

3. How can I share my persuasion successes to inspire my team?

Growth

4. What steps can I take to deepen my understanding of Cialdini's principles?

Bridging Reflection to Action

Persuasion is more than a skill—it's a mindset rooted in service, empathy, and connection. In the next chapter, let's look at Servant Leading Objection Handling.

CHAPTER 13:
Servant Leading Objection Handling

"Empathy is seeing with the eyes of another, listening with the ears of
another, and feeling with the heart of another." — Alfred Adler

Mastering Objection Handling Through Servant Leadership

Objection handling is an essential part of the F&I office, but it's more
than just overcoming customer hesitations. At its core, it's about
practicing **servant leadership**—putting the needs, concerns, and best
interests of the customer first. This chapter explores how empathy,
connection, and understanding customer psychology can turn objections
into opportunities for deeper trust and stronger relationships.

As servant leaders, we don't approach objections with the goal of
"winning" or simply making a sale. Instead, we aim to serve the customer
by addressing their concerns sincerely, guiding them with expertise, and
ensuring they feel valued. Objection handling becomes a chance to
demonstrate that their needs come first, ultimately fostering loyalty,
satisfaction, and long-term success for both parties.

In this chapter, we'll dive deep into the art of objection handling—
combining timeless strategies with modern approaches—to empower
you to address even the toughest concerns while staying true to the
principles of servant leadership.

Understanding Customer Experience

Every customer enters the F&I office carrying the weight of their
unique history. Their perceptions and expectations are shaped by past
interactions, both good and bad. For example, a customer may have
encountered a pushy salesperson aggressively promoting unnecessary

products. Such experiences breed skepticism, often manifesting as objections.

Objections aren't merely challenges—they're windows into the customer's underlying fears, frustrations, or distrust.

Case in Point: The Lingering Frustration

Imagine a customer who recalls the frustration of purchasing a service contract they couldn't utilize due to hidden exclusions. This past disappointment creates resistance to considering similar products. Objections in these instances often stem from emotional barriers rather than outright disinterest.

The Platinum Rule in Action

As mentioned in a previous chapter, the **Golden Rule**—treating others as you would like to be treated—is a timeless principle for building rapport. However, in objection handling, the **Platinum Rule** is even more effective: *Treat others the way they want to be treated.*

To apply the Platinum Rule:

1. **Slow Down and Connect:** Take the time to truly engage with the customer.
2. **Actively Listen:** Hear their concerns without jumping to conclusions.
3. **Acknowledge Their Past Experiences:** Empathize with how those experiences shape their mindset today.

This approach fosters a safe, judgment-free environment where the customer feels heard and understood. By focusing on their needs and preferences, you can uncover their true motivations and address objections with tailored solutions.

The Importance of Empathy

At the core of effective objection handling is empathy. Customers want to feel understood and valued, not rushed or pressured. Empathy allows you to build trust and connect on a deeper level, creating a foundation for productive conversations.

How to Practice Empathy in Objection Handling

When faced with objections, take a moment to pause and ask open-ended questions that invite clients to share their thoughts and concerns. For instance:

1. "Can you tell me more about your previous experience with service contracts?"
2. "What are your main concerns about purchasing additional coverage today?"

These questions accomplish two objectives:

1. They uncover valuable insights into the client's history, fears, and priorities.
2. They demonstrate that you genuinely care about their needs, fostering a sense of trust and partnership.

By practicing empathy, you not only address the immediate objection but also create a positive impression that strengthens the overall relationship.

Reframing the Sales Approach

In the F&I office, success comes from shifting the focus from selling products to helping customers make informed decisions. This subtle yet powerful change in perspective transforms the conversation from transactional to consultative.

Key Principle: Helping, Not Selling

Customers *want* to purchase F&I products; they just don't want to feel pressured into doing so. Your role as an F&I professional is to guide them through the decision-making process, providing clear and honest information tailored to their individual circumstances.

Turning Objections into Opportunities

Rather than seeing objections as roadblocks, view them as opportunities to deepen the conversation and address underlying concerns. Use your expertise to reframe objections into positive discussions. For example:

1. **Customer Concern:** "I don't think I need a service contract."
2. **Reframe:** "I completely understand. A lot of people feel that way initially. Let's talk about how this might help you avoid unexpected costs down the road."

This approach not only eases the client's concerns but also demonstrates your commitment to their best interests, making it more likely they'll see the value in what you're offering.

Digging Deeper: The Root of Objections

To effectively address objections, it's essential to go beyond surface-level concerns and explore the underlying emotions and experiences driving client hesitation. This requires patience, curiosity, and a willingness to dig deeper.

Uncovering Root Causes

Objections are rarely just about the product itself—they often stem from a client's previous negative experiences or fears. Asking probing questions and truly listening to their answers helps uncover these root causes. Examples include:

1. "What concerns you most about this option?"
2. "Have you had a negative experience with a vehicle service contract in the past? If so, what happened?"

By identifying the emotional factors influencing their objections, you can tailor your response to address their specific concerns with empathy and understanding.

Training Through Role-Playing

To prepare your team for real-world objections, incorporate role-playing exercises into your training sessions. Role-playing creates a safe space for F&I professionals to practice active listening, empathy, and strategic objection handling.

Benefits of Role-Playing

1. Simulates diverse customer experiences, preparing your team for a range of objections.
2. Develops confidence and quick thinking in handling challenging scenarios.
3. Provides an opportunity to refine objection-handling techniques based on feedback.

Encourage your team to role-play both sides of the interaction—customer and F&I professional—to gain perspective on client experiences and emotions.

The Foundation of Successful Objection Handling

Handling objections effectively requires a commitment to empathy and an understanding of customer psychology. By recognizing that objections are often rooted in past experiences, F&I professionals can approach clients with patience and compassion.

Key Takeaways

1. **Apply the Platinum Rule:** Treat clients the way they want to be treated.
2. View objections as opportunities for meaningful dialogue, not roadblocks.
3. Focus on understanding, not just overcoming objections.

When we approach objections with empathy and a genuine desire to help, we foster trust, strengthen relationships, and guide clients toward decisions that align with their needs and priorities. This mindset not only enhances the client experience but also elevates the overall performance of the F&I office.

The Art of Listening in the F&I Office

"Most people do not listen with the intent to understand; they listen with the intent to reply." — Stephen R. Covey

Strong communication skills are paramount in the F&I office. However, one of the most underrated skills that can significantly enhance an F&I Manager's effectiveness is the ability to listen. Listening is not merely about hearing words; it involves understanding the underlying needs and concerns of customers. In this section, let's delve into the importance of being a better listener and how it can directly impact your ability to sell F&I products at a higher gross profit.

Understanding the Importance of Listening

Listening is a fundamental component of effective communication. In the context of the F&I office, it allows you to gather valuable insights about your customers' needs and preferences. When customers feel heard, they are more likely to trust you and engage in meaningful conversations about F&I products. This trust can lead to higher sales, increased customer satisfaction, and lasting relationships.

The Listening Process

1. Active Listening

Active listening involves fully concentrating on what the customer is saying rather than just passively hearing their words. It requires you to be present in the moment, making eye contact, nodding in acknowledgment, and providing verbal affirmations such as "I see" or "That makes sense." By demonstrating that you are paying attention, you encourage customers to share more information and feel valued.

2. Empathetic Listening

Empathy goes hand in hand with active listening. It allows you to connect with your customers on an emotional level. When a customer expresses a concern, such as anxiety about the costs of additional coverage, empathizing with their situation helps build rapport. Phrases like "I understand how you feel" or "That's a common concern" validate their feelings and foster a more open dialogue.

3. Clarifying Questions

Asking questions not only shows that you are engaged but also helps clarify uncertainties. For instance, if a customer mentions that they are not interested in purchasing any F&I products, a strategic question like, **"Why is it you prefer to be unprotected?"** invites them to articulate their feelings. This technique isolates the objection, allowing you to address it with logic and common sense.

Techniques to Enhance Listening Skills

Practice Mindfulness

Before starting your day, take a moment to clear your mind. Practicing mindfulness helps you focus on the conversation at hand, free from distractions. This heightened awareness improves your listening ability and sets a positive tone for every interaction.

Avoid Interrupting

It's tempting to jump in with solutions as soon as you hear a concern. Resist this urge. Allow customers to express their thoughts fully before responding. This shows respect and encourages a deeper dialogue, building trust and rapport.

Summarize and Reflect

After a customer shares their thoughts, summarize what you've heard and reflect it back to them. For example, "So, if I understand correctly, you're looking for the lowest rate and you have pre-approval at your credit union?" This not only confirms your understanding but also demonstrates that you value their input.

Building Trust Through Listening

Trust is the foundation of success in the F&I office, where customers are often wary of upselling and hidden costs. Attentive listening creates a safe space for customers to share their concerns openly. When you respond thoughtfully, you establish trust, paving the way for meaningful discussions about F&I products. Customers are more likely to consider options when they feel acknowledged and respected.

Elevating Your Performance Through Listening

Becoming a better listener is a transformative skill for F&I Managers. It allows you to connect with customers on a deeper level, understand their unique needs, and ultimately sell more F&I products at a higher gross profit. By practicing active and empathetic listening, asking clarifying questions, and fostering an environment of trust, you can elevate your performance in the F&I office.

Every conversation is an opportunity to listen, learn, and lead your customers toward the best solutions for their automotive needs. Embrace the art of listening and watch as your sales and customer satisfaction soar.

Selling with Empathy in the F&I Office

"People don't care how much you know until they know how much you care." — Theodore Roosevelt

The Power of Empathy in F&I

The ability to empathize with customers is not just a soft skill; it's a powerful tool for enhancing sales and profitability. Empathy allows us to understand our clients' perspectives and emotional states, fostering trust and connection that can significantly impact their buying decisions. In this section, we'll explore how adopting an empathetic approach can lead to increased sales of F&I products while transforming the overall customer experience.

The Essence of Empathy

Empathy is the capacity to put yourself in someone else's shoes to understand their feelings, thoughts, and experiences. In the F&I office, this means recognizing that every customer comes with their own set of experiences and emotions. Behind every transaction lies a unique story—one that may involve financial concerns, previous negative experiences, or a deep desire for security and peace of mind. Acknowledging this helps tailor your approach to meet their needs effectively.

Understanding the Client's Perspective

1. Listening Actively

Active listening involves engaging in conversations that allow clients to express their concerns and desires. It's more than just hearing their words; it's about observing body language, emotional cues, and what is left unsaid. Insight from active listening can guide your responses and recommendations, making your pitch more effective and genuine.

2. Asking Open-Ended Questions

Open-ended questions encourage clients to share their stories and concerns. For example:

- "What are your main concerns about financing with our dealership?"
- "Can you tell me about your previous experiences with vehicle service contracts?"

Such questions help uncover valuable information about the customer's needs, enabling a more tailored approach.

3. Validating Feelings

Acknowledging and validating customer emotions fosters trust and connection. For instance, if a client expresses feeling overwhelmed by options, respond with: "I can understand how that might feel. It's a big decision, and I'm here to help you navigate it." This validation demonstrates understanding and establishes a stronger rapport.

Serving Clients as Guests in Your Home

A Mindset Shift: Guests, Not Transactions

Imagine welcoming clients into your F&I office as if they were guests in your home. This mindset transforms your approach to one of genuine care and hospitality, encouraging open dialogue and mutual respect.

Creating a Comfortable Atmosphere

Ensure your office is clean, organized, and inviting. Offering small touches like refreshments or ensuring comfortable seating makes clients feel valued and at ease.

Being Attentive and Present

As you would with a guest, give clients your full attention. Set aside distractions, maintain eye contact, and show genuine interest in their concerns. This attentiveness fosters trust and facilitates more productive conversations.

The Profitable Impact of Empathy

Empathy not only enriches the customer experience but also boosts sales and profitability. When clients feel understood and respected, they are more likely to trust your recommendations.

1. Tailored Solutions

Understanding client concerns allows you to offer F&I products that genuinely meet their needs. For example, a customer worried about future repairs might find an exclusionary vehicle service contract appealing when it's presented as a solution to their specific anxieties.

2. Building Long-Term Relationships

Empathetic interactions foster loyalty. Customers who feel connected to you are more likely to return for future purchases and refer friends and family, creating a sustainable business pipeline.

3. Enhancing the Buying Experience

An empathetic approach elevates the buying experience, leading to satisfied customers. Happy clients are more likely to leave positive reviews, recommend your services, and return for repeat transactions.

Empathy as a Core Sales Strategy

Selling with empathy in the F&I office is not just about making a sale—it's about building relationships and creating a positive buying experience. By understanding your clients' perspectives, treating them as valued guests, and consistently demonstrating empathy, you can significantly increase your sales of F&I products and enhance overall profitability.

Empathy is more than a sales tactic; it's a philosophy that enriches both the customer and the F&I professional. By embracing empathy as a core component of your sales strategy, you can transform not only your success but also the lives of those you serve. Let empathy guide your interactions, and watch as trust, sales, and satisfaction soar.

Process is the Most Important Piece to Our Equation in F&I

"Success is the sum of small efforts, repeated day in and day out." — Robert Collier

The Backbone of Success in F&I

In the fast-paced world of F&I, the significance of a structured and defined process cannot be overstated. Processes don't fail—people do. This fundamental truth underscores the need for a robust, repeatable approach that every team member adheres to. From customer engagement to paperwork, a steadfast commitment to the process is the foundation for any high-performing F&I department.

The Necessity of a Robust Process

The Common Denominator of Underperformance

When I travel across the country, visiting finance departments that are struggling to meet their potential, a recurring theme emerges: they lack a well-defined process. Without structure, even the most talented teams cannot consistently deliver results.

A Non-Negotiable Standard

Operating at the highest level in F&I requires a process that is followed 100% of the time. This consistency ensures efficiency, accountability, and improved customer experiences. It's not just a recommendation—it's a requirement.

Identifying the Core Issue: Knowing vs. Doing

Knowing Problems

When performance falters, the first question to ask is whether the issue is a "knowing" problem. Do team members understand the established processes? Have they been trained adequately on both the "how" and the "why?"

1. **Solution:** Comprehensive training is the antidote to knowing problems. Equip your team with the tools, knowledge, and confidence they need to succeed.

Doing Problems

A more complex challenge arises when individuals know the process but fail to implement it—a "doing" problem. This requires deeper investigation:

1. **Honest Conversations:** Why is the process not being followed?
2. **Uncover Root Causes:** Is it a lack of motivation, resistance to change, or something else?

Making Tough Decisions

If an individual cannot or will not align with the process, leaders must be prepared to make difficult decisions about their future within the organization. Maintaining process integrity is non-negotiable for long-term success.

The Role of Leadership in Process Adherence

Training and Empowerment

As leaders, we must ensure our teams are not only trained but also empowered to execute processes with precision. Training should focus on the reasons behind each step, fostering a deeper understanding and buy-in from the team.

Creating a Culture of Accountability

A commitment to the process starts at the top. When leaders model consistency and hold teams accountable, it establishes a culture where adherence to procedures becomes second nature.

Why Embracing Process Is Essential for Growth

For individuals aspiring to rise within their organizations, embracing the process is not optional—it is the cornerstone of advancement. High-performing F&I departments are defined by their dedication to following established procedures. This commitment ensures:

1. **Consistent Performance:** Teams that adhere to the process deliver predictable, repeatable results.
2. **Elevated Sales:** A well-oiled process leads to better customer engagement and increased product penetration.
3. **Sustainable Growth:** Strong processes create a foundation for long-term success.

Let the Process Lead the Way

The key to a successful finance department lies in our ability to embrace and adhere to our processes. While people may falter, a solid process will always guide the way. By fostering a culture of accountability, providing comprehensive training, and addressing "doing" problems head-on, we can ensure consistent performance and drive our organizations to new heights.

Let us remember—processes are the compass that keeps us on course. When we trust in them, success will inevitably follow.

The Power of Accountability

"Accountability breeds response-ability." — Stephen R. Covey

The Foundation of Success

Within the F&I office, accountability stands as a cornerstone of both individual and departmental success. It goes beyond simple oversight—accountability fosters growth, drives excellence, and ensures that processes yield results rather than relying on hope. Let's explore how accountability transforms performance and cultivates a culture of diligence and success.

The Essence of Accountability: Ownership and Precision

Accountability Starts with Ownership

At its heart, accountability is about taking ownership. Having a defined process is vital, but without someone responsible for ensuring adherence to that process, even the best plans can falter. Accountability bridges the gap between establishing procedures and ensuring their consistent execution.

From Discomfort to Growth

Initially, accountability may feel like an uncomfortable imposition. People often resist being held accountable, fearing scrutiny or feeling micromanaged. However, leaning into this discomfort is crucial for growth. Accountability is not about control—it's about fostering a culture of diligence where individuals take their roles seriously and strive for excellence.

The Financial and Cultural Benefits of Accountability

Elevating Performance and Profitability

Teams that embrace accountability consistently outperform their counterparts. Higher sales figures, improved customer satisfaction, and elevated team reputations are direct results of a culture rooted in accountability. This commitment to excellence ultimately boosts the dealership's overall performance.

A Ripple Effect Across Life

Accountability doesn't end in the F&I office. When applied to personal relationships, community engagements, and individual pursuits, it cultivates integrity and fulfillment. By holding ourselves accountable, we inspire those around us and set a standard of excellence.

The Leader's Role in Cultivating Accountability

Modeling Accountability

Leaders must not only hold their teams accountable but also model accountability through their actions. This sets the tone for a culture where every individual understands their role within the larger process and feels empowered to contribute meaningfully.

Creating a Culture of Ownership

Accountability thrives in an environment where team members feel ownership over their roles. Leaders should:

1. Clarify expectations and responsibilities.
2. Provide consistent feedback and support.
3. Celebrate achievements and address shortcomings with fairness and transparency.

Accountability: A Pathway to Achievement

Beyond the F&I Office

Accountability transforms uncertainty into achievement by ensuring processes are followed consistently and correctly. This shift creates measurable results, sustainable growth, and long-term profitability.

Personal and Professional Rewards

While accountability may initially feel uncomfortable, its benefits are far-reaching. Teams perform better, individuals grow stronger, and customers experience better service—all leading to greater fulfillment and success.

The Framework for F&I Success

Throughout this chapter, we've explored principles designed to elevate F&I performance while enhancing the customer experience:

1. **Enhance the Customer Experience:** Use the **Platinum Rule** to treat customers the way they want to be treated.
2. **Learn to Listen:** Understand customer needs and build trust.
3. **Sell with Empathy:** Focus on serving clients, not just selling products.
4. **Serve People:** Build genuine relationships by prioritizing customer interests.
5. **Define Your Process:** Establish a clear and consistent framework.
6. **Embrace Accountability:** Foster a culture of ownership and precision.

Ready for Any Objection

By adopting these principles, you position yourself to handle any objection with sophistication, professionalism, and servant leadership. This approach not only maximizes gross profit but also elevates the buying experience for retail customers, leaving them enchanted with their journey.

Now, let's dive into the strategies and techniques for handling objections with precision and confidence.

Defining and Overcoming Objections

Understanding Objections: Opportunities, Not Rejections

Objections are a natural and inevitable part of the sales process. They reflect the concerns, hesitations, and questions customers have when considering a product or service. These objections might arise from:

1. **Skepticism:** Doubts about the product's value or relevance.
2. **Negative Experiences:** Past issues with similar products or services.

3. **Lack of Information:** Misunderstandings or unanswered questions.
4. **Financial Constraints:** Budget concerns or perceived affordability.

Recognizing objections for what they are—opportunities for deeper engagement—helps you reframe the conversation. Objections are not personal attacks or outright rejections; they are chances to clarify, connect, and build trust with your client.

Setting the Stage for Success: The Pre-Objection Foundation

To effectively handle objections, preparation begins long before they arise. Establishing a foundation of trust and rapport sets the tone for open communication and makes customers more receptive to solutions.

1. Active Listening

Engage fully with the client's words and tone. Show them you value their perspective by avoiding interruptions and providing thoughtful feedback. Active listening communicates respect and signals that their concerns are important.

2. Empathy

Acknowledge and validate their emotions. Saying something as simple as, "I can see why you'd feel that way," fosters connection and opens the door to collaboration. Empathy helps break down barriers and creates a safe environment for dialogue.

3. Clarification

Ask open-ended questions to uncover the true root of the objection. For instance:

1. "Could you share more about your concern with the coverage?"
2. "What is your main hesitation with this option?"

These questions allow clients to articulate their thoughts, giving you insights to address the underlying issue effectively.

4. Solution-Oriented Approach

Once the objection is clearly understood, shift the conversation toward potential solutions. Frame the discussion around how your offering can resolve their concerns and improve their situation.

5. Reinforce Benefits

Circle back to the unique benefits and value your product brings to the table. Help clients see beyond their hesitation by emphasizing the ways your solution aligns with their needs and goals.

Turning Objections into Opportunities

Every objection is a moment to demonstrate your expertise, empathy, and ability to provide value. By addressing concerns thoughtfully and proactively, you not only move closer to closing the deal but also enhance the client's overall experience.

In the next section, we'll dive deeper into specific techniques and real-world examples to master the art of objection handling in the F&I office. These tools will ensure that you are equipped to navigate any concern with confidence and professionalism.

Understanding Objections in the F&I Office

Objections: An Invitation to Engage, not a Door Closing

In the world of F&I, objections are not roadblocks; they are opportunities. It's crucial to understand that not every customer interaction will lead to an immediate "yes." However, an objection doesn't signify failure—it represents a chance to build trust, provide clarity, and demonstrate value.

By viewing objections as an invitation to engage further, you can reframe your approach to these moments. With the right mindset, even the most hesitant customer can be guided toward a decision that benefits both them and your dealership.

The Root Cause of Objections

Most objections in the F&I office stem from a customer's past experiences. A service contract that didn't deliver on promises or a product that seemed unnecessary after purchase can leave lingering doubts. Recognizing this reality allows you to approach objections with empathy and a service-oriented mindset.

Common Sources of Objections:

1. **Previous Negative Experiences:** Dissatisfaction with a past service contract or an unhelpful claims process.

2. **Unmet Expectations:** Feeling oversold or underdelivered in a prior transaction.
3. **Lack of Clarity:** Uncertainty about the product's relevance or value.
4. **Financial Concerns:** Skepticism about whether the expense is justified.

By understanding these root causes, you can address objections at their core, not just their surface expressions.

Objections in the F&I Office: The Essentials to Master

While objections may come in various forms, the truth is that the F&I office encounters a limited set of recurring objections. By mastering the art of addressing these specific concerns, you can significantly improve your close rates and customer satisfaction.

Building a Foundation for Objection Handling:

1. **Structured Process:** Having a clear and consistent approach ensures you never feel unprepared when faced with resistance.
2. **Accountability:** Regularly review your responses to objections and seek to refine them based on outcomes.
3. **Empathy and Service:** Always approach objections with the mindset of solving problems and serving the customer's best interests.

Later in this chapter, we'll dive into the specific objections most encountered in the F&I office, offering strategies and scripts to address them effectively. Mastering these will empower you to turn hesitations into agreements, one conversation at a time.

The Mindset for F&I Success

Cultivating Passion and Confidence

To truly excel in F&I, you must first cultivate a genuine passion for the products and services you offer. This enthusiasm acts as a cornerstone of your success, as it not only inspires confidence in your clients but also demonstrates your commitment to their needs. When clients sense your belief in the value of F&I products, they are more likely to trust your recommendations.

Passion is contagious. When you genuinely believe in the benefits of service contracts, GAP insurance, or extended warranties, your energy and conviction naturally influence the customer's perception. This enthusiasm becomes a powerful tool in building rapport and overcoming objections.

Turning Setbacks into Growth Opportunities

Not every interaction will end in a sale, but each one presents a learning opportunity. When a client decides not to purchase, take the time to reflect and evaluate your approach. Ask yourself:

1. **What could I have done differently?** Did I fully understand the client's concerns and address them effectively?
2. **Was I truly aligned with the client's needs?** Did I offer solutions that genuinely fit their unique situation?
3. **Did I communicate the value effectively?** Were the benefits of the product clearly articulated in a way that resonated with the client?

This practice of introspection is essential for growth. By analyzing your interactions, you can identify areas for improvement and refine your techniques, ensuring you are better prepared for future conversations.

The Art of Mastering Objections

Mastering objections is not just about closing deals; it's about building trust and fostering relationships with your clients. Approaching objections with empathy and a structured process allows you to transform hesitations into meaningful conversations.

Key Pillars for Overcoming Objections:

1. **Embrace Objections as Opportunities:** View objections as a natural part of the sales process and an invitation to connect with the client on a deeper level.
2. **Employ a Structured Approach:** Follow a consistent framework to address concerns methodically and effectively.
3. **Reflect and Adapt:** Use every interaction—successful or not—as a stepping stone for personal and professional growth.

Elevating Your F&I Performance

By embracing a mindset rooted in passion, reflection, and a commitment to your clients' best interests, you can elevate your F&I performance to new heights. Remember, every objection is a stepping stone toward building trust and strengthening relationships.

Success in F&I is about more than selling products— it's all about enhancing the buying and ownership experience for the retail customer. By aligning your mindset with these principles, you'll not only overcome objections but also position yourself as a trusted advisor and leader in the industry.

The Most Common Objections in F&I

Objections are inevitable in the F&I office, but they are not insurmountable. Here are the most common objections and their underlying causes:

1. **"I can't afford the payment with the F&I products."** This objection often stems from concerns about budget constraints and financial pressure.
2. **"I do not see the value in the F&I products."** This is typically due to a lack of understanding about the benefits and how they apply to the customer's unique needs.
3. **"I purchased F&I products in the past and had a bad experience."** This objection reflects a breach of trust based on previous negative experiences.
4. **"I was told never to purchase F&I products."** Customers influenced by advice from others may approach the discussion with preconceived notions and skepticism.
5. **"I am going to take the risk and self-insure."** This objection reflects a mindset of risk tolerance or an overestimation of their ability to cover future expenses.

Setting the Stage: The Transition into the Menu

A seamless and confident transition into the menu presentation is critical for addressing these objections effectively. This is where all the groundwork you've laid—listening, empathy, and rapport-building—comes into play.

The Importance of a Strong Transition

Your transition sets the tone for the menu presentation. A well-executed transition helps put the client at ease and establishes a collaborative atmosphere. This is not the time to apply pressure; rather, it's the moment to reinforce trust and convey that your goal is to help, not sell.

My Proven Technique

I use a technique that has consistently helped me ease my clients into the menu presentation. It's simple, yet highly effective:

1. **Start with Transparency:** Begin by explaining what the menu presentation is and why it's important. For example:
    i. "This is where I get to show you all the tools available to protect your investment and give you peace of mind for the future."
2. **Use Inclusive Language:** Position yourself as a partner in their decision-making process.
    i. "Let's walk through this together to make sure you have all the information you need to make the best choice for you."
3. **Establish a Positive Tone:** Reassure the client that this is an opportunity, not an obligation.
    i. "My goal is simply to show you the options available so you can decide what makes sense for your situation."

By setting the stage with transparency, inclusion, and positivity, you create an environment where objections can be addressed constructively. With the right transition and approach, objections become opportunities to provide value and build trust.

In the following sections, we'll explore how to address each of the common objections in detail, turning them into moments of connection and growth.

Diffuse the Bomb

Setting the Tone with Confidence and Transparency

When transitioning into the menu presentation, one of the most powerful techniques is to diffuse the customer's apprehension before it even arises. Using straightforward language and addressing their unspoken concerns head-on can establish trust and lower resistance.

The Script:

"Mr./Mrs. Customer, I am about to go over a few vehicle protection options with you. The last thing I'm going to do is sit here and try to sell you something that you don't need or want. We do not do that here at ABC Motors. These membership options are designed to enhance your ownership experience while protecting your budget."

Why This Technique Works

1. **Reduces Customer Defensiveness** Many customers walk into the F&I office with their guard up, expecting a high-pressure sales pitch. This script immediately disarms them by addressing their fears directly.
2. **Positions You as a Partner** By emphasizing that you're not there to push unnecessary products, you position yourself as an advisor who genuinely cares about their needs, not just a salesperson.
3. **Frames the Products as Valuable Additions** Highlighting that the products "enhance the ownership experience while protecting their budget" shifts the conversation to focus on the customer's benefit, rather than the dealership's profit.

Delivering the Script Effectively

1. **Use a Calm and Friendly Tone:** This isn't just about the words you say; how you say them matters. Speak with sincerity and confidence.
2. **Maintain Eye Contact:** This builds trust and reinforces your credibility.
3. **Pause for Effect:** After delivering the script, pause briefly to allow the customer to process your words and relax.

Building Trust Through Transparency

This technique not only diffuses tension but also sets the stage for a collaborative conversation. By proactively addressing potential objections, you create an environment where the customer feels comfortable asking questions and engaging in an open dialogue about the options presented.

With this foundation of trust, the rest of your menu presentation will flow more smoothly, allowing you to focus on matching the right products to the customer's unique needs.

Feel-Felt-Found: A Time-Tested Technique for Objection Handling

The **Feel-Felt-Found** technique has stood the test of time because of its simplicity and effectiveness in overcoming objections. By empathizing with the customer's concerns, relating to their experience, and providing a new perspective, this approach allows you to transition smoothly into addressing their objections.

How It Works

1. Acknowledge the Customer's Feelings
   i. "I know how you feel..." This opening line demonstrates empathy, signaling to the customer that you understand their concern.
2. Relate Through Personal Experience
   i. "I felt the exact same way..." Sharing a similar experience shows that you're relatable and credible. It also reassures the customer that their concerns are valid.
3. Pivot to a Solution
   i. "Here's what I found out..." This is your opportunity to introduce a solution or reframe the customer's perception with a story or insight that addresses their objection.

Example Scenario: Service Agreement Concerns

Customer Objection:

"I bought a service agreement in the past, and it never covered anything."

Response Using Feel-Felt-Found:

"Mr./Mrs. Customer, I know how you feel because I felt the exact same way on a previous purchase of mine. I purchased a service contract for my Chevy truck, and every time I was in the service department for a repair, the contract conveniently never covered anything. It was more than frustrating, so I can totally relate to you."

"Here's what I found out: service contracts today are much different than they used to be. The contract I offer has exclusionary coverage, which means it covers almost everything except what's specifically listed as excluded. You won't find yourself in the same predicament that you and I both experienced in the past."

Why It's Effective

1. **Builds Empathy:** The customer feels heard and validated.
2. **Establishes Credibility:** Sharing your own experience makes you relatable and trustworthy.
3. **Reframes the Objection:** Transitioning into a solution helps shift the customer's mindset from resistance to consideration.

The Key Elements of Feel-Felt-Found

1. I Know How You Feel
   i. Demonstrates empathy and understanding.
   ii. Validates the customer's concerns, creating a sense of trust.
2. I Felt the Exact Same Way
   i. Establishes relatability and positions you as someone who's been in their shoes.
   ii. Reinforces that you're not just selling but genuinely care about their experience.
3. Here's What I Found Out
   i. Provides a logical pivot to present a solution.
   ii. Offers a chance to weave in a brief but impactful story that helps close the sale.

The Power of Storytelling in Automotive Sales

Feel-Felt-Found taps into the power of storytelling, which is one of the most persuasive tools in sales. By sharing a relatable and concise story, you humanize the sales process and create a connection with the customer. This approach doesn't just address objections; it turns them into opportunities to build trust and close the deal effectively.

In every objection scenario, the **Feel-Felt-Found** technique serves as a bridge between resistance and resolution. It's a tool every F&I professional should have in their arsenal, capable of transforming even the toughest objections into successful outcomes.

The Power of Storytelling in Automotive Sales Presentations

"The most powerful person in the world is the storyteller. The storyteller sets the vision, values, and agenda of an entire generation that is to come." — Steve Jobs

It's About Connection

Sales presentations in the F&I office are not just about facts and figures; they're about connection. Storytelling is a timeless tool that bridges the gap between transactional selling and meaningful engagement. It appeals to our innate human desire for connection and makes the value of F&I products come alive. In this section, we'll explore how to harness the art of storytelling to captivate customers, overcome objections, and boost gross profits.

The Psychology of Storytelling

Why Stories Work

Humans are wired for stories. From bedtime tales to blockbuster movies, narratives engage our emotions and make information memorable. The magic of storytelling lies in its ability to lower defenses and captivate attention. When you say, *"Let me tell you a quick story,"* the dynamic changes. Suddenly, you have the customer's undivided attention, opening the door for meaningful dialogue.

Turning Transactions into Relationships

Stories transform a cold pitch into a warm conversation. For instance, instead of merely presenting features, share a story about a customer who benefited from the same product. Did they save thousands on repairs with a service contract? Did a GAP policy rescue them during an unforeseen accident? These real-life narratives demonstrate value in a relatable way, fostering trust and connection.

The Emotional Impact of Storytelling

Evoke Emotions, Drive Decisions

While logic informs, emotions decide. A story about a family avoiding financial strain due to a service contract doesn't just inform—it moves. By creating an emotional connection, storytelling can guide customers to envision themselves benefiting from your products.

Sell Solutions, Not Products

Through storytelling, you're not selling F&I products; you're selling peace of mind, security, and confidence. When customers see how your offerings solve real-life problems, they are more inclined to say yes.

Crafting Stories That Sell

1. Know Your Audience

Every customer has unique concerns. Tailor your stories to address their specific objections or priorities. For example:

1. Concerned about high repair costs? Share a story about a customer who saved big with a service contract.
2. Unsure about GAP insurance? Recall a customer who avoided financial ruin because of it.

2. Be Authentic

Authenticity builds trust. Share genuine experiences—whether they're your own or from previous clients. Customers can sense insincerity, so ensure your stories are real and relatable.

3. Keep It Concise

Time is precious, so keep your stories focused and purposeful. A concise story with a clear message is far more impactful than a lengthy one that veers off track.

4. End with Purpose

Every story should lead to a call to action. Conclude with how the product can address the customer's needs, creating a seamless transition to closing the sale.

Storytelling in Practice: An Example

Scenario:

A customer hesitates to purchase a service contract, citing a tight budget.

Story:

"I completely understand where you're coming from. I had a customer, Susan, who felt the same way. She was on a tight budget and decided against a service contract for her SUV. Six months later, her transmission failed, and the repair bill was over $3,000. Susan came back and told me she wished she had taken the service contract because it would have covered the entire repair. Since then, she's never purchased a car without one. I share this because I don't want you to experience what Susan did."

Key Benefits of Storytelling

1. **Enhances Engagement:** Stories capture attention and keep customers invested.
2. **Builds Trust:** Authentic narratives establish credibility and relatability.
3. **Increases Retention:** Customers remember stories long after facts fade.
4. **Boosts Profitability:** Emotionally engaged customers are more likely to invest in F&I products.

Actionable Steps to Master Storytelling

1. **Develop a Story Bank:** Collect impactful stories from your experiences or those of colleagues. Categorize them based on common objections or concerns.
2. **Practice Delivery:** Rehearse your stories to ensure they are concise, compelling, and relevant.
3. **Focus on Outcomes:** Highlight the positive impact the product had on the customer in your story.
4. **Seek Feedback:** After sharing a story, gauge the customer's response and refine your approach accordingly.

Master storytelling and become a servant leader

Storytelling is more than a sales technique—it's a way to connect, inspire, and convert. By weaving narratives into your F&I presentations, you can elevate the customer experience, address objections with empathy, and close more deals at higher gross profits. Every product you sell has a story waiting to be told. Master this art, and you'll not only enhance your performance but also leave a lasting impression on every customer you serve.

Quote to Remember:

"Facts tell, but stories sell." — Unknown

Let's Talk About Cash Deals

Does the Perfect Car Fairy Exist?

Why are VSC (Vehicle Service Contracts) sales notoriously lower on cash transactions? Does the perfect car fairy bless the vehicles of those who pay in cash, shielding them from repairs and inconvenience? Of course not. Yet, many F&I Managers approach cash deals with hesitation—or worse, indifference.

If we focus solely on PVR and not the customer, failure is inevitable. Cash customers deserve the same care, enthusiasm, and opportunity as any other client. The payment method should not dictate the level of service or the effort to offer protection.

The Challenge of Cash Transactions

Old Habits Die Hard

F&I Managers often dread cash deals, skipping interviews, bypassing menus, and failing to build value into the product. This is a surefire recipe for missed opportunities, resulting in a big fat zero and a hit to PVR. Why does this happen? Because there's no payment manipulation, and old-school "repair scare" tactics fall flat with savvy customers.

A New Perspective

It's time to reframe the narrative. Cash deals come with unique advantages:

1. **No CIT Log Hassles:** Funds are collected on the same day.
2. **Less Paperwork:** Transactions move faster, freeing up time.
3. **Cash Customers Have...Cash:** They can invest in protection; you just need to ask for it.

Bringing Value to Cash Customers

Universal Customer Needs

All customers—cash or finance—share common goals:

1. Maximize the use and enjoyment of their vehicle.
2. Minimize aggravation.
3. Reduce total ownership costs.

The service contract is tailor-made to fulfill these needs. It:

1. Covers repairs, eliminating out-of-pocket expenses.
2. Provides rental cars, ensuring convenience.
3. Enhances resale value by offering an "exit strategy."

Breaking Down the Math

Shifting Their Perspective

Cash customers often weigh the cost of the service contract against their expected repair expenses, leaving them uncertain. It's your job to change the conversation:

1. **Introduce the Exit Strategy:** A service contract positions customers to negotiate from strength when trading or selling their vehicle.
2. **Highlight Long-Term Savings:** Keeping the car another year avoids depreciation, sales tax, and financing costs.
3. **Emphasize Peace of Mind:** Explain how the service contract ensures they're never out-of-pocket for repairs or inconvenienced by breakdowns.

The Key: Custom-Tailored Presentations

Leverage the Interview

Cash customers deserve the same thoughtful approach as finance customers. Use the interview to gather insights about their driving habits, long-term plans, and concerns. Tailor your menu presentation to align with these insights, building trust and demonstrating value.

Maintain Enthusiasm

Bring the same level of passion and professionalism to every transaction. Cash customers are no exception. A positive, energetic approach is contagious and helps convey the importance of your products.

The Power of the Service Contract

1. **For Long-Term Savings:** Service contracts save cash customers from surprise repair bills, preserving their budget.
2. **For Negotiating Power:** When it's time to sell or trade, a service contract adds value, giving them flexibility.
3. **For Overall Satisfaction:** The happiest customers are those who never have to pay for a repair or face inconvenience.

Key Takeaways

1. **Avoid Bias:** Treat cash customers with the same care and enthusiasm as any other client.
2. **Change the Conversation:** Reframe cash transactions as value propositions.
3. **Emphasize the Service Contract:** Highlight its role in convenience, savings, and resale value.
4. **Tailor Presentations:** Use insights from the interview to create personalized solutions.
5. **Stay Passionate:** Enthusiasm and professionalism are key to building trust and selling more.

The Service Contract is a Value-driven Solution

The perfect car fairy doesn't exist, but the service contract does. By offering tailored, value-driven solutions to cash customers, you can protect their investment, enhance their experience, and increase your sales. The happiest customers are those who never have to worry about repairs—and you have the power to make that happen.

Exit Strategy Concept: A New Approach to Selling Service Contracts

"The most valuable lessons come from thinking differently and acting deliberately." — Unknown

Revolutionizing the Value Buyer's Experience

In this segment, my goal is to challenge your perspective and ignite fresh ideas. Let's explore a different approach to selling service contracts that resonates particularly well with the value buyer. The **Exit Strategy Concept** is designed to combat the "hard no" objection, providing a pathway to overcome resistance and close the sale with confidence.

This strategy is not about pressure—it's about preparation, communication, and delivering tailored solutions. Let's dive into the core principles that make the Exit Strategy Concept so effective.

The Foundation of the Exit Strategy Concept

To execute this approach at the highest level, F&I Black Belts adhere to these essential steps:

1. Get Involved Early

The best impressions are made early in the transaction.

1. Be visible and proactive on the showroom floor or alongside your sales manager.
2. Show urgency to serve rather than sell, fostering trust and rapport from the start.

2. Communicate at the Highest Levels

Strong communication is the backbone of success.

1. Collaborate with your desk and sales team to gather valuable insights about the customer.

2. Remember, the sales manager is the F&I Manager's best ally—they are the architects of the dealership experience.

3. Conduct a Robust Customer Interview (or Conversation)

Gathering detailed information about the customer's needs, preferences, and concerns is essential.

1. Listen actively and document key points that will guide your tailored solutions.

4. Deliver a Robust Factory Warranty Presentation

Every transaction—new or used—deserves a compelling warranty presentation.

1. Highlight the benefits of protection and align them with the customer's needs.

5. Tailor a Menu Presentation Specifically for the Client

A one-size-fits-all approach won't work.

1. Use the information you've gathered to create a customized menu presentation that speaks directly to your client's priorities.

Why These Steps Matter

Skipping any of these critical steps puts you at a disadvantage, especially when dealing with value buyers. These are the customers who scrutinize every dollar and often enter the conversation with skepticism. By following this process, you:

1. Build trust and rapport early.
2. Position yourself as a solution provider rather than a salesperson.
3. Tailor your approach to address the unique concerns and objections of the value buyer.

Key Takeaways

1. **Engage Early:** Make a great first impression and show your commitment to service.
2. **Communicate Effectively:** Collaborate with your team to gather insights and align strategies.
3. **Conduct Meaningful Conversations:** Use the customer interview to uncover needs and objections.

4. **Present with Precision:** Ensure warranty and menu presentations are detailed and tailored.
5. **Follow the Process:** Adhering to the Black Belt Road to Sale is non-negotiable for success.

The Exit Strategy Concept is a Mindset

The exit strategy concept is more than a closing technique; it's a mindset. By approaching each transaction with preparation, communication, and a customer-first attitude, you can turn even the toughest objections into opportunities. For the value buyer, it's not just about selling a service contract—it's about creating a solution they can't resist. Implement this strategy, and watch your results soar.

Transition After the "Hard No"

Handling the Initial Decline with Empathy and Curiosity

When a customer quickly declines coverage, it's important to stay composed and seek to understand their reasoning. By asking the right question and following up with empathy, you can shift the conversation and uncover the root cause of their objection.

F&I Manager: "Mr. or Mrs. Customer, you were quick to decline the coverage. What is the main reason you prefer to be unprotected?"

Possible Customer Responses and Your Next Steps

Customers will typically respond with one of the following objections:

1. "I don't ever buy any extra protection."
2. "I do not believe in warranties."
3. "I am going to self-insure."
4. "I was told never to buy them."
5. "I had a warranty on my last vehicle, but nothing was covered."

Each of these objections provides an opportunity to shift the dialogue and connect with the customer on a deeper level. This is where the **Feel-Felt-Found** approach, paired with storytelling, becomes incredibly powerful.

Feel-Felt-Found: Turning Objections into Opportunities

Empathize:

"Mr. and Mrs. Customer, I know how you feel because I have felt the exact same way."

Relate:

"Here's what I have found out. The coverage available today is so much better than the coverage available a decade ago."

Your Story: Relating Through Personal Experience

F&I Manager's Story:

"Let me tell you a quick story. Growing up, my father told me to never purchase any extended protection. His father, my grandfather, told him to never purchase extended protection either. Why? Because my grandfather and father bonded over working on cars together. It's how they connected. My father and I used to bond the same way—under the hood of a car.

"But here's the thing: times have changed. Vehicles today are nothing like the ones my grandfather and father worked on. Technology has taken over. What used to be simple and affordable repairs are now complex and incredibly expensive. Today, my dad and I bond in different ways—like at the bar (my mom hates that, by the way).

"The point is vehicles today are more expensive to repair than ever before. That's why coverage like this has become such a vital part of ownership—it's not just about peace of mind; it's about protecting your investment and your budget."

Why This Approach Works

1. **Empathy:** By expressing that you understand how the customer feels, you disarm their defenses and show that you're on their side.
2. **Relatability:** Sharing your own experience builds a bridge of trust and positions you as someone who genuinely understands their perspective.
3. **Education:** Highlighting how vehicle technology and repair costs have evolved frames the service contract as a necessary solution for modern ownership.

4. **Engagement:** Storytelling captures attention and conveys the value of the product in a memorable way.

Key Takeaway

The transition after the "hard no" is not about pushing harder but about connecting deeper. By asking thoughtful questions, empathizing with the customer's concerns, and sharing relatable stories, you can turn objections into opportunities for meaningful conversations and, ultimately, successful sales.

Crystal Ball Transition: Turning Uncertainty into Confidence

Setting the Stage

Handling objections often requires a shift in perspective, and the **Crystal Ball Transition** is a powerful technique to engage customers who are uncertain about the value of a service contract. By presenting a hypothetical scenario, you guide the customer to see the logic and practicality of the coverage in a way that feels relatable and rational.

The Transition Dialogue

F&I Manager: "Mr. or Mrs. Customer, if you and I had a crystal ball and we knew you would have $6,000 in repairs, and you could buy a service contract for $3,000, you would go ahead and purchase the service contract, right?"

Customer: "Well, yes, of course!"

F&I Manager: "Exactly. We all would. But here's the thing—I don't think you're going to have $6,000 in repairs. In fact, if my service contract worked the way you think it does, I wouldn't buy it either.

"The good news is, mine works completely differently, and I can't wait to show you how."

Why This Works

1. **Logical Appeal:** The crystal ball scenario taps into the customer's logical reasoning. By framing the decision in terms of potential savings versus costs, it leads the customer to recognize the value of the service contract on their own.

2. **Acknowledges Skepticism:** By admitting you wouldn't buy a subpar product either, you validate the customer's concerns. This disarms their skepticism and opens the door for a constructive conversation.
3. **Builds Curiosity:** Ending with *"I can't wait to show you how mine works"* piques the customer's interest, creating an opportunity to explain the benefits of the service contract in detail.

Practical Tips for Success

1. **Use a Confident Tone:** Deliver the transition with enthusiasm and assurance to instill confidence in your customer.
2. **Be Ready with Details:** Follow up with a thorough explanation of how your service contract differs from others they may have encountered.
3. **Incorporate Personalization:** Tailor your explanation to the customer's specific concerns or vehicle history to make the benefits more tangible.

Key Takeaway

The **Crystal Ball Transition** transforms uncertainty into curiosity, creating an open dialogue about the value of a service contract. By using this approach, you address objections head-on while fostering trust and paving the way for a meaningful, solution-focused conversation.

The $10,000 Question: Framing Value and Generating Interest

Introduction

Objection handling in the F&I office often requires a compelling approach that aligns with the customer's priorities. The **$10,000 Question** is a strategic way to introduce the benefits of a service contract by positioning it as a high-value opportunity. This method sparks curiosity and primes the customer to be receptive to your presentation.

The Dialogue

F&I Manager: "I have a quick question for you. If I had a program where I could enhance your factory warranty from 3 years/36,000 miles to 8 years/120,000 miles, provide a rental car with roadside assistance, and put $10,000 in your savings account, would you be interested in that service contract?'"

Customer: "Well, yes, that sounds amazing!"

F&I Manager: "Of course, you would. And that's why I have something I want to show you. I think you're going to like it."

Why This Works

1. **Captures Attention:** By framing the benefits as a significant enhancement—both in coverage and financial impact—you immediately grab the customer's attention.
2. **Simplifies Value:** Highlighting the tangible benefits (extended warranty, rental car, roadside assistance, and perceived financial security) breaks down the offering into relatable, customer-centric terms.
3. **Builds Anticipation:** Ending with *"I think you're going to like it"* creates a sense of excitement and curiosity, encouraging the customer to engage with the next part of your presentation.

Key Elements for Success

1. **Confident Delivery:** Speak with conviction and positivity to make the offer sound as compelling as possible.
2. **Tailored Presentation:** Be ready to follow up by presenting a customized menu or explanation that aligns the service contract with the customer's specific needs.
3. **Maintain Engagement:** Transition seamlessly into your pitch while ensuring the customer feels involved and respected.

Takeaway

The **$10,000 Question** positions the service contract as a no-brainer decision by equating its benefits to real, impactful value. It primes the customer to see the service contract not just as an expense, but as an investment in convenience, protection, and financial peace of mind.

Entry to the Exit Strategy Close: Shifting Focus from Entry to Exit

In the F&I office, shifting the customer's mindset from the immediate transaction to the long-term value of their purchase can be transformative. The **Entry to the Exit Strategy Close** is designed to help customers see beyond the initial cost and focus on their overall ownership experience, particularly how it impacts their financial future.

The Dialogue

F&I Manager: "Let me be abundantly clear, I am not trying to sell you something you don't need. I used to be the type of person who declined this kind of coverage—until a few years ago when my mindset shifted. I started to look beyond the entry of the deal and into the future.

"Most of my customers are just like you—they want the best price, lowest rate, and overall best deal. Some will even drive 200 miles to save $200. But here's the thing: in focusing so much on the entry of the deal, they often lose sight of something equally important—their exit from the vehicle."

The Pivot: Understanding Depreciation

F&I Manager: "Let me ask you this: what do you think is the biggest expense when buying a new vehicle? It's not the interest rate or even the insurance—it's depreciation.

"Take a $50,000 car, for instance. In three years, it's worth about $25,000. Another three years, and it's down to $12,500. Depreciation is unavoidable, but how we manage it makes all the difference."

The Exit Strategy Close

F&I Manager: "Now, let me ask you this: if this vehicle serves your needs and makes you happy, would you consider keeping it for just one more year beyond your initial plan? Let's take a moment to explore what that could look like and how the right coverage can help you make that decision without hesitation."

Why This Works

1. **Reframes the Narrative:** It shifts the focus from the "entry" (initial purchase price) to the "exit" (long-term ownership benefits and resale value).
2. **Introduces Logic and Emotion:** The concept of managing depreciation appeals to the logical side, while the idea of keeping a beloved vehicle for longer connects on an emotional level.
3. **Sets the Stage for the Close:** By asking if they'd consider keeping the vehicle longer, you open the door to presenting coverage options to protect that decision.

Key Elements to Execute

1. **Clear and Relatable Language:** Avoid industry jargon and speak in terms the customer can easily understand.
2. **Use Visuals if Possible:** A quick depreciation chart or numbers breakdown can help drive the point home.
3. **Tie It Back to the Product:** Position service contracts and other F&I products as tools to mitigate depreciation and extend the vehicle's usability.

Takeaway

The **Entry to the Exit Strategy Close** redirects the customer's attention from short-term savings to long-term value. By helping them see the big picture and framing F&I products as essential for their vehicle's future, you build trust, provide value, and pave the way for a successful close.

Let's Do Some Math: The Long-Term Financial Advantage

Introduction

When it comes to deciding on a service contract, nothing speaks louder than numbers. Helping customers see the long-term financial impact of their choices can turn a "no" into a confident "yes." This approach connects the dots between protecting their investment and maximizing their savings over time.

The Breakdown: Turning Numbers into Value

F&I Manager: "Let's break this down together. Your monthly payment is $750, and you're financing it over six years. Now, let's look at what happens when you invest in my 8/120 service contract.

"This service contract covers your vehicle for eight years or 120,000 miles—longer than your loan term. This gives you the flexibility to keep the vehicle for an extra year or two without worrying about costly repairs. Let's do the math."

The First Year of Savings

F&I Manager: "In year seven, after your loan is paid off, you're no longer making that $750 monthly payment. Instead, you can deposit that into your personal savings account. That's $750 times 12 months, which equals **$9,000 saved** in just one year.

"Now let's add in the first-year depreciation of a new vehicle. On average, that's around $6,000. By holding onto your vehicle longer, you avoid taking that hit on a brand-new car. That brings your total savings to **$15,000.**"

Sales Tax Savings

F&I Manager: "But wait, there's more! On a new vehicle, you're looking at an average sales tax of around $2,000. By keeping your vehicle instead of trading prematurely, you avoid paying that tax again. That brings your total savings to **$17,000.**"

Negotiating Power at Trade-In

F&I Manager: "Because you have a service contract, you get to trade in this vehicle on your terms—not when the car decides. Let me explain what I mean. Without a service contract, vehicles nearing 100,000 miles often start to have issues, forcing customers to trade earlier than planned. This exposes you to additional depreciation and sales tax expenses.

"With the service contract, you're in a position of strength. When you bring your vehicle in for a trade, my sales manager will offer you more because it's fully covered. If we take two identical cars, one with warranty coverage and one without, which do you think is worth more? Exactly—the one with the warranty.

"We're seeing about a **$1,500 difference** in trade-in value between vehicles in 'fair' condition and those in 'good' condition with warranty coverage. That brings your total savings to **$18,500**."

What If You Keep It Longer?

F&I Manager: "Now, let's say you decide to keep the vehicle for two extra years beyond your loan term. Those savings multiply. Imagine two additional years of no car payments and no major repair costs because of the service contract. Your financial flexibility increases significantly, allowing you to save even more or put that money toward other goals."

The Value Proposition

By laying out the math in this way, the conversation becomes less about selling a product and more about demonstrating value. Customers see how the service contract isn't just an added expense—it's an investment in their financial future, providing peace of mind and substantial savings.

Close the Conversation

F&I Manager: "The beauty of this approach is that you're not just protecting your vehicle—you're protecting your budget, your savings, and your peace of mind. Let's take a closer look at the service contract and see how it fits your needs. What do you think?"

Key Takeaways

1. Focus on the **long-term financial benefits** of the service contract.
2. Highlight how the service contract provides flexibility and negotiating power at trade-in.
3. Demonstrate the savings in a tangible, step-by-step manner.
4. Reinforce the emotional value: less stress, fewer surprises, and smarter financial decisions.

With this structured approach, customers are more likely to see the value in the service contract and make an informed, confident decision.

The VSC: A Latte a Week for Peace of Mind

Introduction

When it comes to investing in a vehicle service contract (VSC), the value is unparalleled. Imagine all the protection and peace of mind you receive—for the cost of just a latte a week. Let's explore how to address common objections with empathy and professionalism, starting with an objection many F&I Managers encounter: interest rates.

Objection: "That interest rate you're offering is too high."

Response Framework

Acknowledge and Empathize:

"I completely understand why you would say that. These are challenging times economically. Inflation is at an all-time high, and unfortunately, we are in a high-interest-rate environment."

Educate and Explain:

Your interest rate is determined by several factors, including the following:

1. Loan-to-Value (LTV) Ratio
2. Duration of the Loan Term
3. Credit Score
4. Age of the Vehicle

Reassure and Offer Solutions:

"One of my responsibilities here at the dealership is to secure the most attractive financing package available for you. Based on the current structure of this deal, this is the best rate we can offer. However, if you're open to adjusting the terms—such as shortening the loan duration or putting down additional cash—I'd be happy to reach out to the bank and renegotiate on your behalf."

Why This Approach Works

1. **Acknowledgement Builds Trust:** By empathizing with the customer's concern, you validate their feelings and open the door for constructive dialogue.
2. **Transparency Fosters Understanding:** Explaining the factors that determine interest rates educates the customer, reducing confusion and skepticism.
3. **Offering Solutions Demonstrates Service:** Proactively suggesting alternatives like a shorter term or larger down payment shows a willingness to help, which builds goodwill and enhances the customer's experience.

Closing the Loop

After addressing the objection and explaining the options, pivot back to the value of the deal. Reiterate the benefits of the service contract and how it fits into their overall financial plan. This ensures the focus remains on the customer's needs and the value you're providing.

By combining empathy, education, and actionable solutions, you can handle even the toughest objections with professionalism, ensuring a positive customer experience while driving results for the dealership.

Objection: "The rate is high. I saw a bank advertising a lower rate."

Response Framework

Acknowledge and Empathize:

"I hear this feedback from customers all the time, and I completely understand your concern."

Educate on Bank Advertisements:

Banks and credit unions often advertise their absolute lowest rates to attract attention. What they don't always explain is that these rates are usually tied to very specific conditions, such as:

1. Short-term loan durations.
2. Significant down payment requirements.
3. An 800+ credit score or higher.

Reassure with Dealer Advantages:

"Here at [Dealership Name], we have preferred relationships with multiple lending institutions. This allows us to provide you with a variety of options tailored to your specific needs."

Build Confidence in Your Offering:

"99 times out of 100, we're able to place our customers in a much better financial position than if they pursued a loan independently. With our expertise and access to competitive rates, we'll ensure you get the best package for your circumstances."

Why This Approach Works

1. **Acknowledgment Creates Rapport:** Recognizing the customer's concern establishes trust and shows you're on their side.
2. **Education Dispels Misconceptions:** By explaining the fine print behind bank advertisements, you provide clarity and position yourself as a reliable guide in the lending process.
3. **Highlighting Advantages Builds Value:** Emphasizing your dealership's relationships with lenders and ability to offer tailored solutions makes your financing option more appealing.

Pivot to the Close

After addressing the objection, bring the focus back to the bigger picture: "Ultimately, our goal is to ensure you leave here with the best overall value—both in terms of your vehicle and your financial peace of mind. Let me run through a couple of scenarios for you to make sure we're hitting all the marks."

By combining empathy, transparency, and reassurance, you not only handle the objection effectively but also reinforce the value of working with your dealership.

Objection: "The term is too long."

Response Framework

Empathize and Acknowledge:

"I completely understand why that would concern you. It's a legitimate point and something I considered myself when purchasing my last vehicle."

Highlight Common Customer Goals:

Most of our customers prioritize a few key things when purchasing a vehicle:

1. The greatest use and enjoyment.
2. The least amount of aggravation.
3. The lowest total cost.

Reframe the Objection:

"By extending the term by another year, you gain the benefit of a lower monthly payment. This can be a helpful way to navigate today's economic environment, where we're experiencing record levels of inflation."

Provide Flexibility and Reassurance:

"Remember, this is a simple interest loan, so you always have the option to pay it off early if your situation allows. Extending the term gives you flexibility without locking you into higher monthly payments that could strain your budget."

Address Changing Ownership Habits:

"Additionally, we're seeing more customers planning to keep their vehicles longer than ever before due to the rising costs of new cars. A slightly longer term can give you financial breathing room while aligning with this trend."

Why This Approach Works

1. **Empathy Creates Connection:** Acknowledging the concern shows you're on the customer's side and not just trying to sell them on your terms.
2. **Reframing Shifts Perspective:** Positioning a longer term as a tool for financial flexibility helps the customer see it as a benefit rather than a drawback.
3. **Providing Solutions Builds Trust:** By mentioning the ability to pay off the loan early, you're demonstrating flexibility and removing a potential sticking point.

Pivot to the Close

"My best advice would be to extend the term for now to take advantage of the lower payment and maintain flexibility in your budget. If things change down the line, you always have the option to pay the loan off early, giving you the best of both worlds. Let's go ahead and see how this works for your overall plan."

This approach not only addresses the objection but also reassures the customer that they retain control, fostering trust and confidence in the decision.

Objection: "I do not want the service contract."

Response Framework

Empathy and Inquiry:

"No problem at all. You were quick to decline the coverage offered to you. Can I ask, what is the main reason you prefer to be unprotected?"

Address the Customer's Objection:

(**Customer**: "I don't believe in warranties.") "I completely understand where you're coming from. I've been hesitant in the past to purchase extended protection on certain items myself."

Make a Relatable Comparison:

"Let me ask you something. I noticed you have a newer smartphone. I also noticed you have a case and a screen protector to protect it. If you're like me—and I think you are—you probably have insurance on your phone as well, just in case it gets damaged."

Reframe the Value:

"Now, let's think about this for a moment. You're spending around $15 per month to cover a $1,000 device. Why wouldn't you spend just $40 per month to protect a $40,000 computer on wheels?"

Pause for Reflection:

"When you think about it that way, doesn't it make sense to have peace of mind knowing you're covered for unexpected repairs?"

Why This Approach Works

1. **Empathy First:** By acknowledging the customer's concern and sharing a similar hesitation, you create a connection that reduces resistance.
2. **Relatable Analogy:** Comparing the service contract to phone insurance makes the concept relatable and positions the investment as logical.

3. **Highlighting Value Over Cost:** Breaking down the cost into a small monthly amount compared to the potential risk reframes the decision as an affordable safeguard.

Pivot to the Close

"Ultimately, the decision is yours, but the peace of mind knowing you're covered for major repairs is something that many of my customers really appreciate. Let's go over how this coverage works in more detail, so you have all the information you need to decide."

This response combines empathy, logic, and relatability to address the objection while gently guiding the customer toward reconsidering the service contract.

Objection: "I have a mechanic in the family."

Response Framework

Empathy and Personal Connection:

"Having a mechanic in the family can truly be a blessing. My grandfather was a mechanic, and growing up, he and my dad worked on trucks together. By default, my dad and I spent a lot of time working on vehicles together too."

Humor to Build Rapport:

"We used to bond under the hood of the car. Now, because of technology, we bond at the bar. My mom hates that."

(Pick up your phone here when saying, "because of technology," to visually reinforce the point.)

Transition to Value:

"The great news for you is this: With the service contract, you can still have your family mechanic service the vehicle if they carry the proper certifications. Not only will they get paid for their work, but you'll also have peace of mind knowing the repairs are covered."

Reframe the Benefit:

"It's a win-win situation for you and your mechanic. You get to keep your trusted family connection while protecting your budget from unexpected repair costs."

Why This Approach Works

1. **Personal Storytelling:** Sharing a relatable and lighthearted story creates a connection and puts the customer at ease.
2. **Reinforcing Trust:** Highlighting that the family mechanic can still be involved reassures the customer that they're not giving anything up.
3. **Win-Win Framing:** Positioning the service contract as a mutual benefit adds value and shifts the focus from cost to convenience and protection.

Pivot to the Close

"Ultimately, the service contract gives you flexibility to keep your trusted mechanic involved while covering the big-ticket items that can arise. Let's review the details so you can decide what's best for you and your family."

This approach blends empathy, humor, and logic to address the objection while maintaining a positive tone and reinforcing the value of the service contract.

Objection: "I'm going to decline the service contract. I'll purchase one later before the factory warranty expires."

Response Framework

Acknowledge the Customer's Plan:

"You absolutely can wait to purchase the service contract later, and I understand why that might feel like a good option."

Introduce Cost Implications:

"However, that decision could be an expensive one. Right now, your vehicle is brand new, and you're able to lock in terms and pricing designed for a brand-new car. The moment you drive off the lot, it becomes a used vehicle, and the cost of a service contract will increase."

Explain Favorable Terms for Early Purchase:

"Additionally, purchasing today gives you access to more favorable terms, such as longer coverage options and lower deductibles. By waiting, you risk losing out on these benefits and paying a higher price later."

Position Immediate Action as Cost-Saving:

"If you're even remotely considering the service contract, I'd strongly recommend securing it now to take advantage of the best pricing and coverage available. Plus, you're protected from day one, rather than waiting until something happens."

Why This Approach Works

1. **Acknowledges the Customer's Perspective:** By validating their thought process, you avoid creating a confrontational tone.
2. **Highlights Financial Impact:** Emphasizing the cost increase and less favorable terms later creates a sense of urgency.
3. **Reframes the Value Proposition:** Positioning early purchase as a smarter financial move shifts the focus from "buying now" to "saving later."

Pivot to the Close

"Ultimately, the decision is up to you, but most of my customers appreciate the peace of mind that comes from locking in better terms and pricing upfront. Let's go over the details together so you can make the most informed decision."

This response combines validation, education, and urgency to guide the customer toward purchasing the service contract now.

Objection: "I don't want my credit pulled because I do not want my credit score to go down."

Response Framework

Acknowledge the Concern:

"I completely understand your concern, and the last thing we want to do is put you in a situation where your credit score is negatively impacted."

Educate on Credit Pulls:

"Here's the good news: A single credit inquiry from us will not cause a noticeable drop in your credit score. Credit scoring models account for rate shopping in the auto industry. Even if multiple inquiries are made within a short time frame, they are typically grouped together and treated as one inquiry by the credit bureaus."

Address Common Misconceptions:

"Your credit score might be negatively impacted if you were to visit 10 dealerships and have all of them pull your credit and send it to multiple banks. However, that's not how we operate."

Reassure Professionalism:

"Our Finance department specializes in lending, and with just one credit report, we can pinpoint the right lender for your situation. This streamlined process ensures you get the best options without unnecessary credit inquiries."

Why This Approach Works

1. **Validates the Customer's Concern:** Acknowledging the worry builds trust and lowers their defenses.
2. **Provides Clarity:** Educating the customer on how credit pulls work removes the fear of significant score reductions.
3. **Reinforces Expertise:** Highlighting the finance department's professionalism reassures the customer that their credit will be handled responsibly.

Pivot to the Close

"You're in great hands, and I can assure you that we'll only pull your credit when it's absolutely necessary and in a way that minimizes any impact. Let's take a look at the best options for you."

This response educates, reassures, and keeps the conversation moving toward a resolution.

Objection: "I don't want any of those extras."

Response Framework

Acknowledge the Customer's Position:

"I completely understand, Mr./Mrs. Customer. When I hear someone say this, it's often because of a bad experience in the past or simply not seeing the value at the time."

Connect with Current Realities:

"With today's economy and inflation rates being as high as they are, many customers who declined protection in the past are now realizing the importance of being covered. In fact, some of our most satisfied customers were initially hesitant but found significant value in these options."

Invite Exploration:

"Allow me to show you our suite of products and explain the benefits they offer. I think you'll find that some of them are tailored to meet your specific needs and concerns. My goal isn't to sell you something you don't need but to ensure you're protected in a way that makes sense for you."

Why This Approach Works

1. **Validates the Customer's Hesitation:** Acknowledging their resistance builds rapport and shows you're listening.
2. **Addresses Current Realities:** Linking the conversation to economic factors makes the protection relevant and timely.
3. **Focuses on Education, Not Pressure:** By offering to explain the benefits, you position yourself as a consultant, not just a salesperson.

Pivot to the Close

"Let's take a quick look at the options. Even if you decide not to proceed, you'll have the peace of mind of knowing exactly what's available to you."

This response maintains professionalism, educates the customer, and keeps the door open for further discussion.

Objection: "I don't want the service contract because I had a bad experience."

Response Framework

Empathize and Relate:

"I can completely understand how you feel, Mr./Mrs. Customer. I had a similar experience myself. I remember buying a service contract years ago, and every time I went to the service department, it seemed like the repairs I needed weren't covered. It was beyond frustrating."

Highlight Improvements in Today's Contracts:

"The good news is that the service contracts we offer today are a completely different story. They've evolved significantly to better meet the needs of our customers."

Explain the Value:

"The service contract I'm offering you now is an exclusionary policy, which means it covers everything on the everything on the vehicle except for the small list of exclusions and maintenance. Plus, it comes with added benefits like rental car coverage and roadside assistance. It's designed to ensure you're never caught off guard by unexpected repair costs."

Reinforce Financial Protection:

"This service contract is also a great way to guarantee you'll never pay more than you should for repairs in the service department. It's about protecting your investment and giving you peace of mind."

Why This Approach Works

1. **Empathy Builds Trust:** Sharing a personal experience helps the customer feel understood and less alone in their hesitation.
2. **Focuses on Progress:** By highlighting how service contracts have improved, you shift their perspective from the past to the present.
3. **Offers Clear Benefits:** Explaining exclusionary coverage and added perks makes the contract tangible and valuable.

Pivot to the Close

"Let me show you exactly what this service contract covers and how it could benefit you. I think you'll be pleasantly surprised by how much peace of mind it can offer."

This approach transitions the conversation from hesitation to consideration, keeping the focus on addressing their concerns while emphasizing value.

Objection: "I do not want Tire & Wheel"

Response Framework

Acknowledge and Ease Resistance:

"No problem at all, Mr./Mrs. Customer. I completely understand where you're coming from."

Ask a Thought-Provoking Question:

"Quick question—why take on the risk of a wheel or tire repair yourself when you can transfer that risk to insurance for less than two lattes per month?"

Highlight Common Risks:

"When you think about the debris and potholes on our roads, it's astonishing how frequently they cause damage. That's exactly why we offer this coverage. Our Wheel and Tire program ensures you and your family stay on the road without unexpected repair costs."

Explain the Benefits Clearly:

Here's what the program includes:

1. Full coverage for repairs to damaged tires and rims.
2. Cosmetic repairs to alloy wheels, like fixing curb damage. I'll admit, my spouse has a knack for hitting curbs, and I'm grateful we have this protection!
3. 24/7 roadside assistance for added peace of mind.
4. Enhanced trade-in value. Our used car manager rewards vehicles with undamaged rims, so this coverage could save you money in the long run."

Create Urgency and Value:

"There's never been a more critical time to ensure our vehicles are protected, especially with today's road conditions and rising repair costs. The real question is—would you like all these benefits for less than two lattes per month?"

Why This Approach Works

1. **Eases Initial Resistance:** Starting with "No problem" makes the customer feel heard and reduces tension.
2. **Uses a Relatable Comparison:** Framing the cost in terms of "two lattes per month" makes it seem minimal and manageable.
3. **Provides Tangible Value:** Specific examples of what the policy covers (e.g., curb damage, trade-in value) make the benefits easy to visualize and compelling.
4. **Injects Humor and Personal Connection:** Sharing a relatable story about curb damage adds personality and relatability to the pitch.

Pivot to Close

"Let me show you exactly how this coverage works and how it could benefit you. I think you'll see why so many of our customers choose to protect their investment with this program."

This response shifts the focus from the objection to the benefits, making the customer reconsider the value of the coverage.

Objection: "I am going to pass on the windshield coverage."

Response Framework

Acknowledge and Relate:

"I completely understand. To be honest, I used to feel the same way and would never have considered purchasing windshield protection in the past."

Share Personal Experience and Shift Perspective:

"However, today, I won't purchase a vehicle without this coverage. Let me tell you why—it's not just about protecting the glass; it's about ensuring safety, convenience, and saving money in the long run."

Explain the Unique Benefits:

*"This program does so much more than replace or repair a chipped windshield:

1. **Strengthens the Glass:** It's treated to make it more resistant to chips and cracks caused by flying debris.
2. **Covers Repairs and Replacements:** If a rock chip does happen, you're covered, whether it needs a repair or a full replacement.
3. **Addresses Costly Recalibrations:** Modern factory windshields often require recalibration of advanced safety features when replaced, which can be very expensive. This program includes that."*

Safety Features of the Program:

"It's not just about protection—it also enhances safety:

1. **Reduces Glare:** The chemical treatment reduces glare, making nighttime driving easier and safer.
2. **Hydrophobic Coating:** Rainwater runs off the windshield effortlessly, improving visibility in poor weather conditions."*

Highlight Affordability and Value:

"All these benefits come at less than the price of a coffee per week. For me, the peace of mind and the added safety features make it a no-brainer."

Why This Approach Works

1. **Relates to Customer Doubts:** Sharing a personal story or initial hesitation builds trust and relatability.
2. **Emphasizes Practical Benefits:** By focusing on safety, convenience, and cost savings, the pitch resonates with logical and emotional concerns.
3. **Positions the Program as Essential:** Highlighting modern challenges like recalibration costs and hydrophobic advantages shows how this is a necessity, not a luxury.
4. **Frames Cost as Minimal:** Comparing the cost to a weekly coffee simplifies decision-making and minimizes financial objections.

Pivot to Close

"This coverage has truly made a difference for so many of our customers. Let me show you exactly how it works—it's something I think you'll really appreciate once you see it in action."

This response makes windshield protection feel indispensable while easing resistance by focusing on its tangible and safety-oriented benefits.

Objection: "I'm going to pass on the service contract because it still has the factory warranty."

Response Framework

Acknowledge and Validate:

"I understand why you might feel that way. It makes sense to think the factory warranty provides all the coverage you need for now."

Highlight the Long-Term Perspective:

"You mentioned that you plan on keeping this vehicle longer than three years. That's a great choice! With that in mind, you have a unique opportunity to extend the factory coverage now into a 7-year program, which aligns perfectly with the loan term you selected."

Emphasize Protection and Peace of Mind:

"The last thing anyone wants is to face an unexpected repair after the factory warranty expires. With the vehicle service contract, you can avoid those surprise expenses and enjoy a seamless ownership experience for years to come."

Simplify the Cost Decision:

"For less than the price of a cup of coffee per week, you'll gain all the amazing benefits of a comprehensive vehicle service contract. It's a small investment for significant peace of mind."

Why This Approach Works

1. **Validates Customer Concerns:** Acknowledging their initial thoughts builds rapport and avoids resistance.
2. **Positions the Service Contract as a Long-Term Solution:** Tying the extended coverage to the customer's plans to keep the vehicle emphasizes its relevance.
3. **Highlights Cost-Effectiveness:** Breaking down the cost into manageable terms ("a cup of coffee per week") makes it seem minimal compared to the benefits.
4. **Focuses on Avoiding Future Hassles:** Stressing unexpected repair costs taps into the customer's desire to avoid inconvenience and financial strain.

Pivot to Close

"This is truly about giving you a worry-free ownership experience. Wouldn't it be great to have the confidence that no matter what happens, your vehicle is protected?"

This approach aligns the service contract with the customer's long-term goals while addressing potential objections in a relatable and practical way.

Objection: "What if I never use the warranty?"

Response Framework

Acknowledge and Build Perspective:

"Mr./Mrs. Customer, that's a fair question and a common concern. Let me put it this way—sometimes the best insurance is the one you never have to use."

Relatable Analogy:

"I noticed you own your home. When was the last time you pulled into your driveway and were upset that your house wasn't on fire? Of course, you weren't. You pay for home insurance, hoping nothing ever happens, but you'd never think of going without it, right? It's about protecting your assets and having peace of mind."

Highlight the Warranty's Added Benefits:

"My service contract does the same thing for your vehicle. It protects your asset and ensures that if a major repair is necessary, you're covered without financial stress. Plus, when it's time to trade, having coverage can increase your resale value, putting you in a position of strength."

Point Out Flexibility:

"Even if you never use it, this coverage is transferable to the next owner, which increases your trade-in value. And if you decide to cancel it at that point, you'll be reimbursed for the unused portion. It's truly a win-win."

Why This Approach Works

1. **Acknowledges the Customer's Concern:** It validates their question and shows understanding.
2. **Creates a Relatable Analogy:** Comparing it to home insurance makes the logic tangible and easy to grasp.

3. **Shifts the Focus to Asset Protection:** Emphasizes the service contract's role in preserving and enhancing the value of their vehicle.

4. **Highlights Flexibility:** Offering the option to transfer or cancel reassures the customer of the contract's value, even if unused.

Pivot to Close

"The peace of mind alone makes it worth considering, but the additional trade-in value and flexibility really seal the deal. Let's go ahead and make sure you're protected—just in case."

This response reframes the objection into a discussion about value and flexibility, making it easier for the customer to see the long-term benefits of the service contract.

Objection: "I'll do your offer if you offer a discount."

Response Framework

Acknowledge the Customer's Value Recognition:

"I greatly appreciate that you see the value in this product. In fact, 9 out of 10 of my customers are just like you—they understand the importance of protecting themselves and their investment."

Explain Pricing Transparency:

"I would love to discount this product for you, but here's the thing: we price all our products with small profit margins to ensure they're competitive and provide maximum value right from the start. That's why we don't deviate from the price—it's already structured to deliver the best benefits at the fairest cost."

Offer Customization Instead of a Discount:

"The great news is, we can customize this product to better fit your budget. For example, we can adjust the terms, mileage limits, or deductible to bring the cost down while still providing you with excellent protection. Let me show you a few tailored options."

Why This Approach Works

1. **Validates the Customer's Desire for Value:** Shows appreciation for their willingness to consider the product and affirms their reasoning.
2. **Creates Transparency:** Explains why the pricing is firm in a way that feels fair and reasonable.
3. **Shifts the Focus to Flexibility:** Redirects the conversation to finding a customized solution instead of a discount.

Pivot to Close

"Let's take a look at some of these options. I'm confident we can find something that works for you while still giving you the protection and peace of mind you're looking for."

This approach maintains the integrity of your pricing structure while providing the customer with alternatives that address their budget concerns.

Objection: "I don't want the key replacement."

Response Framework

Empathize with Their Hesitation:

"I completely understand why you've declined this coverage in the past—I felt the same way. In fact, I used to think the same thing about key replacement programs."

Explain the Shift in Perspective:

"Here's why I've changed my mind on key replacement coverage: Over the past three years, I've noticed more claims in our service department for lost keys. It made me curious, so I did some research."

Share Relevant Data:

"According to a study I found, the average person loses up to nine items per day, with car keys often at the top of that list. Factors like stress and fatigue make it easier to misplace items like keys, even for the most organized individuals."

Highlight the Value of the Program:

"With the cost of keys and programming being as high as $800 per key, the key replacement program provides incredible value. It allows you to make a claim once per year, covering the full cost of a replacement key and programming. That's peace of mind for what is now an essential—and expensive—part of your vehicle."

Why This Approach Works

1. **Acknowledges the Customer's Initial Stance:** Validating their previous choice prevents the response from feeling confrontational.
2. **Builds Credibility Through Data:** Sharing a relatable statistic adds weight to your recommendation and frames the coverage as a practical solution.
3. **Demonstrates Financial Protection:** Explains the financial benefits of the program, focusing on how it safeguards against an increasingly common and costly issue.

Pivot to Close

"It's one of those coverages that most of my customers don't think they need—until they do. I'd hate for you to find yourself in that situation without the protection this program provides. Let's go ahead and add it to ensure you're fully covered."

This approach connects with the customer's logical and emotional concerns, making the value of the program clear and relatable.

Objection: "I have a budget, and I can't pay any more per month. I'll just stay with my original payment."

Response Framework

Empathize With Their Concern:

"I completely understand, and I respect the importance of sticking to a budget. We all have financial limits—some tighter, some more flexible—but everyone appreciates knowing their payment remains consistent."

Introduce the Concept of Fixed Payments:

"Here's what I've found with many of my customers: they want their payment to remain the same month after month, without any surprises. Choosing to stay unprotected may initially feel like a safe decision, but it could expose you to unexpected expenses that disrupt your budget."

Illustrate With a Scenario:

"Let's look at this practically: If your payment is $650 with the service contract, it remains $650 each month, even if you encounter a covered repair. Because we've set you up with a disappearing deductible, your out-of-pocket costs are minimal. On the other hand, if you decline the service contract, your $650 payment could suddenly become $1,250 or more if a $600–$700 repair comes up. Without protection, unexpected repairs turn a fixed payment into a variable expense, which can throw off even the most carefully planned budgets."

Key Points to Reinforce

1. **Predictability Over Uncertainty:** Customers appreciate consistency. Highlighting how the service contract ensures fixed monthly costs makes it an easier decision.
2. **Disappearing Deductible:** Reinforce the value of minimizing repair expenses while keeping their payments stable.
3. **Protection Against the Unknown:** Frame the service contract as a safeguard against unexpected financial strain, keeping their monthly obligations predictable.

Pivot to Close

"The best way to protect your budget is to invest in the service contract. It's peace of mind knowing your payment won't suddenly skyrocket due to an unforeseen repair. Let's go ahead and include it so you can enjoy the stability and security that comes with full protection."

This approach addresses the customer's budget concerns while presenting the service contract as the practical solution to avoid financial surprises.

Why Purchase a Service Contract?

"The best preparation for tomorrow is doing your best today." — H.
Jackson Brown Jr.

Service Contracts are Key to Profitability

The vehicle service contract (VSC) is one of the most valuable products offered in the F&I office. It not only provides significant benefits to the customer but also plays a pivotal role in elevating dealership profitability and customer satisfaction. By mastering the art of selling service contracts, F&I professionals can impact their PVR (Per Vehicle Retail) dramatically and enhance the overall customer experience. In this section, we'll explore why the VSC is an indispensable offering for both the dealership and the customer and how to effectively present it.

The Value of a Service Contract

Selling a service contract isn't just about pushing a product—it's about delivering peace of mind and long-term value. Customers today are informed, demanding, and often impatient. They expect transparency and efficiency in the F&I office. A well-presented VSC not only meets these expectations but exceeds them.

Key Benefits of a Vehicle Service Contract

1. **Comprehensive Exclusionary Coverage:**
   i. Modern service contracts offer extensive coverage, protecting nearly every component of the vehicle.
2. **Convenience Over Cost:**
   i. Customers will pay more to avoid being inconvenienced by unexpected repairs.
3. **Trade-In Advantage:**
   i. Vehicles with service contracts often fetch higher trade-in values, giving customers a negotiating edge.

4. **Peace of Mind:**
    i.   The VSC eliminates the stress of surprise repair costs, allowing customers to enjoy their vehicles worry-free.
5. **Exit Strategy for Ownership:**
    i.   A service contract provides flexibility, enabling customers to keep their vehicles longer while saving thousands in depreciation, sales tax, and interest.
6. **Nationwide Usability:**
    i.   Service contracts are honored across the country, ensuring customers are covered no matter where they are.
7. **Faster Claims Processing:**
    i.   Advances in technology mean claims are approved and processed more quickly than ever before.
8. **Enhanced Customer Satisfaction:**
    i.   As service contracts evolve, they offer better experiences, leading to happier and more loyal customers.
9. **Long-Term Coverage Options:**
    i.   Extended coverage ensures the vehicle is protected well beyond the factory warranty.
10. **Combats Depreciation:**
    i.   The VSC is a powerful tool to combat the unavoidable decline in vehicle value over time.
11. **Empowers Future Purchases:**
    i.   With savings from a service contract, customers may pay cash or make substantial down payments on their next vehicle.
12. **Mitigates Problematic Situations:**
    i.   Should a vehicle become problematic, the VSC allows the customer to make calm, informed decisions without being rushed.
13. **Protection in Service departments:**
    i.   A VSC ensures customers are not overcharged or taken advantage of during repair visits.

The Art of the Menu Presentation

A successful F&I professional tailors their menu presentation based on customer conversations and personality types. This approach builds trust, aligns with the customer's needs, and ultimately leads to greater penetration of additional products. Here's how to elevate your menu presentation:

1. **Get Involved Early:**
   i. Connect with the customer early in the process to understand their preferences and needs.
2. **Discover Personality Types:**
   i. Adjust your presentation style based on whether the customer is detail-oriented, analytical, or emotionally driven.
3. **Structure Customized Packages:**
   i. Design packages that maximize value for the customer while meeting dealership goals.
4. **Deliver With Transparency:**
   i. Present products sincerely and clearly, avoiding any semblance of a "sales pitch."

The Power of Slowing Down

In our fast-paced industry, slowing down can seem counterintuitive. However, taking the time to connect with customers and make a lasting impression can make all the difference. A thoughtful, engaging approach not only increases sales but also ensures customer loyalty. **Remember:**

1. The customer who buys a service contract today is more likely to return to your dealership for their next vehicle.
2. That same customer is also more likely to purchase another service contract in the future.

Key Takeaways

1. The service contract provides unmatched value to both the customer and the dealership.
2. A well-structured and personalized menu presentation is key to maximizing product penetration.
3. Slowing down and connecting with customers builds trust, loyalty, and long-term success.
4. The impression you leave with a customer can shape their perception of your dealership and influence their future purchasing decisions.

Action Steps

1. **Commit to Tailored Presentations:**
   - i. Make every menu presentation customer-centric and aligned with their specific needs.
2. **Focus on Benefits, Not Just Features:**
   - i. Highlight the real-life impact of a service contract—convenience, savings, and peace of mind.
3. **Adopt a Transparent Approach:**
   - i. Ensure your communication is sincere, clear, and free from pressure tactics.
4. **Create a Memorable Experience:**
   - i. Strive to leave a positive and lasting impression during every customer interaction.

Closing Thought

"We don't sell service contracts; we sell peace of mind, convenience, and financial empowerment."

Mastering the art of presenting and selling service contracts is not only about increasing PVR—it's about delivering exceptional value and forging lasting relationships with your customers. Let's rise to the challenge and redefine what it means to serve in the F&I office.

When Value Exceeds Price: The Modern Approach to F&I Success

"People don't buy products—they buy solutions to their problems." —
Zig Ziglar

The traditional principle that customers will purchase F&I products when value exceeds price has stood the test of time, but the modern automotive landscape calls for an evolved understanding of this concept. In today's F&I office, it's not just about demonstrating value—it's about cultivating trust and fostering relationships. This chapter explores the layered dynamics of value, trust, and relationships and how they can revolutionize your approach to selling F&I products.

The Three Phases of Value in F&I Sales

1. **When Value Exceeds Price.** At its core, this phase reflects a logical assessment by the customer. They may see the benefit of your products, but logic alone often fails to close the deal. Without an emotional connection, the decision remains transactional, and the likelihood of purchase diminishes.
2. **When Value Exceeds Price and Trust is Established.** Trust acts as a catalyst in the buying process. When a customer likes and somewhat trusts you, they feel more secure in their decision-making. This level of trust encourages them to move beyond consideration and into action.
3. **When Value Exceeds Price, and a Strong Relationship is Cultivated.** The ultimate driver of F&I success is a relationship built on genuine rapport. When customers truly like and trust you, they view you as a partner rather than a salesperson. This environment fosters confident buying decisions, increasing both the frequency and quality of purchases.

The Shift in the Automotive Landscape

Modern retail customers are informed, empowered, and proactive. They approach the car-buying process with research and expectations, seeking transparency and value. While they *want* to buy F&I products, they recoil at the feeling of being sold to. Recognizing this distinction is the cornerstone of effective sales in today's F&I environment.

Strategies for Building Trust and Rapport

1. **Be Likable:**
    i. Smile, be approachable, and engage with customers as individuals.
    ii. Use positive body language and maintain eye contact to create a welcoming atmosphere.
2. **Demonstrate Genuine Interest:**
    i. Actively listen to customers' concerns and needs.
    ii. Use open-ended questions to invite them to share more about their expectations and preferences.
3. **Provide Tailored Solutions:**
    i. Avoid cookie-cutter pitches. Customize your recommendations based on what the customer has shared with you.
4. **Communicate Transparently:**
    i. Be upfront about costs and benefits. Transparency fosters trust and diminishes skepticism.
5. **Follow Through:**
    i. Build credibility by doing what you say you will do. Even small commitments, like promptly following up on questions, reinforce trust.

Transforming the Sales Process

The modern F&I approach moves away from hard-selling tactics and toward consultative conversations. This shift involves:

1. **Active Listening**: Truly hear and understand what your customers need.
2. **Empathy**: Acknowledge their concerns and validate their emotions.
3. **Education**: Equip customers with the knowledge to make informed decisions.

4. **Solution Orientation**: Focus on solving problems rather than selling products.

Creating a Comfortable Environment

Customers are more likely to open and engage when they feel comfortable. To foster this environment:

1. **Use Relatable Language**: Avoid technical jargon or overly complicated explanations.
2. **Be Approachable**: Encourage dialogue rather than delivering monologues.
3. **Address Concerns Directly**: Show that you care about resolving their doubts.

Key Takeaways

1. **Value Alone Isn't Enough**: Emotional connection and trust are essential for closing deals.
2. **Modern Customers Are Informed**: Tailor your approach to meet their expectations for transparency and value.
3. **Rapport Is Key**: Building relationships transforms the transaction into a collaborative experience.
4. **Provide Solutions, Not Sales Pitches**: Customers are more likely to buy when they feel you are helping them meet their needs.

Action Steps

1. **Invest in Building Rapport**: Spend time getting to know your customers before diving into product presentations.
2. **Emphasize Trustworthiness**: Deliver on promises and be honest about product details and pricing.
3. **Focus on the Relationship**: View every interaction as an opportunity to foster a long-term connection with your customer.

Closing Thought

When the value exceeds the price, trust is established, and relationships are nurtured, F&I sales transform into opportunities to genuinely serve your customers. By focusing on their needs, addressing their concerns, and building lasting connections, you ensure success— not just for the dealership but for the customers who rely on you to protect their investment. Embrace this approach and watch your F&I performance thrive.

Objection Handling as a Pillar of Servant Leadership

Objection handling in the F&I office is not just about refining your sales techniques; it's about embodying the principles of **servant leadership**. When you truly serve your customers—listening to their concerns, validating their feelings, and offering solutions that genuinely meet their needs—you transform the interaction from a sales pitch to a partnership.

As servant leaders, our goal is not to push products but to empower customers to make informed decisions. By focusing on the customer's well-being, we build trust and credibility, showing them that their needs come before our goals. This mindset not only leads to higher customer satisfaction but also aligns with the long-term vision of sustainable success.

Here's how objection handling ties back to servant leadership:

1. **Empathy First:** By actively listening and empathizing, you demonstrate that you understand and care about the customer's concerns.
2. **Building Trust:** Addressing objections transparently and authentically reassures customers that you are their advocate, not just a salesperson.
3. **Guiding, Not Pushing:** Servant leaders provide information and options, empowering customers to choose what's best for them rather than pressuring them into decisions.

When viewed through the lens of servant leadership, objections are no longer obstacles—they're opportunities to serve. They're chances to connect with customers, understand their unique perspectives, and tailor solutions that genuinely enhance their ownership experience.

As you step into your next customer interaction, remember the core principles of this chapter: listen with intent, approach objections with empathy, and serve your customers by putting their needs above all else. By adopting this mindset, you won't just handle objections effectively— you'll leave a lasting impression as a trusted advisor, a dedicated professional, and a true servant leader. This is how you not only close deals but also open doors to long-term success and meaningful customer relationships.

SECTION 4:

The Servant Leader's Path to Legacy

CHAPTER 14:
Entry-Control-Execute

"The best leaders don't climb to the top alone—they lift others as they rise." – Unknown

In Brazilian Jiu-Jitsu, every match starts with a calculated dance of strategy and skill. Stepping onto the mat, I'm reminded that success isn't just about physical ability—it's about the discipline to master a process. This lesson extends far beyond the mat into the F&I department. Over the years, I've realized that the principles of Jiu-Jitsu—Entry, Control, and Execute—are also the cornerstones of effective F&I management.

This isn't just about winning; it's about serving others. In both arenas, true success comes from empowering those around us—our customers, our teams, and ourselves. In this chapter, I'll explore how these three phases guide not only transactions but also servant leadership in action.

Entry

In Jiu-Jitsu, entry is your first move—positioning yourself to execute your strategy effectively. In the F&I office, entry begins at the earliest touchpoint with the customer. Servant leaders understand that building trust and rapport early in the process isn't about personal gain; it's about creating a foundation of mutual respect and understanding.

To achieve this, F&I Managers must be proactive. Partnering with the sales team is crucial, as customer experience begins long before they reach our office. A seamless handoff requires alignment, open communication, and a shared commitment to service. The earlier we're involved, the more we can enhance a customer's journey, ensuring their expectations are not just met but exceeded.

Example in Action: A customer starts asking about financing early in the sales process. Instead of waiting until they're handed off to the

F&I office, an F&I Manager steps in, introduces themselves, answers initial questions, and creates a sense of trust. This early involvement sets the tone for a smoother, more transparent transaction.

Control

Control is about setting the pace and direction of the interaction—whether on the mat or in the dealership. In Jiu-Jitsu, this means neutralizing your opponent's movements; in F&I, it means guiding the customer and the sales team through a cohesive, value-driven process.

For the sales team, this involves ongoing training and support. Empowering them with the knowledge to confidently address financing and product questions isn't just a task—it's an act of leadership. A well-prepared team ensures consistency, reduces friction, and ultimately serves the customer better.

With the customer, control involves clear communication and managing expectations. When we listen actively and respond thoughtfully, we demonstrate respect for their time and needs. Servant leadership here means prioritizing their best interests—ensuring they feel informed, valued, and empowered to make confident decisions.

Example in Action: A dealership organizes weekly training sessions where F&I Managers share best practices with the sales team, improving alignment and equipping them to handle customer inquiries more effectively. As a result, the handoff to F&I becomes smoother, saving time and boosting customer confidence.

Execute

Execution is where preparation meets action. In Jiu-Jitsu, this is the moment to finish a submission; in F&I, it's the finalization of the deal. But execution isn't about closing for the sake of profit—it's about delivering a solution that genuinely benefits the customer.

When trust and rapport are established, execution becomes a natural conclusion rather than a hard sell. Servant leaders recognize that success lies in enhancing the customer's experience. We create lasting value by presenting products that align with their needs and offering guidance rather than pressure.

Example in Action: A customer comes into the F&I office uncertain about the products being offered. Instead of pushing the product, the F&I Manager takes time to understand their concerns, explains the benefits clearly, and connects the solution to the customer's specific needs. The result? A confident purchase decision and a satisfied customer.

Summary

The flow of **Entry, Control, and Execute** is both a strategy for success and a philosophy of service. It's about positioning ourselves to serve, guiding with intention, and delivering solutions that prioritize the customer's best interests. These principles, when embraced with a servant's heart, drive excellence in the F&I office and beyond.

Key Takeaways

1. **Entry:** Early involvement in the sales process lays the foundation for trust and success.
2. **Control:** Guiding the transaction through clear communication and preparation ensures consistency and value.
3. **Execute:** Delivering genuine solutions enhances both the customer experience and dealership success.
4. **Servant Leadership:** Elevating others—customers, teams, and peers—creates lasting impact.

Action Steps

For F&I Managers

1. Collaborate with the sales team early in every transaction. Build alignment to ensure seamless customer experiences.
2. Approach customers with empathy and a genuine desire to solve their problems, reflecting servant leadership values in every interaction.

For Dealership Teams

1. Reinforce a culture of service by recognizing and rewarding behaviors that prioritize customer satisfaction over immediate sales goals.
2. Share feedback with the F&I team to continually improve processes, fostering a collaborative, growth-oriented environment.

For Individual Professionals

1. **Lead by Example:** Demonstrate servant leadership by actively helping colleagues, even when it doesn't directly benefit your immediate role.
2. Seek opportunities to mentor less experienced team members, sharing knowledge about the Entry-Control-Execute framework.

How to Apply This

In the F&I Office

Use the **Entry-Control-Execute** framework to guide every transaction. Begin early, maintain alignment, and execute with precision and care.

Across the Dealership

Adopt a unified approach where every department works collaboratively to serve the customer. Consistency is the key.

In Your Daily Practice

Live the servant leadership mindset: Serve others first, and your success will follow.

Practical Tools for Success

1. **Self-Reflection Prompts:**
    i. Am I positioning myself early enough to positively impact outcomes?
    ii. How well am I listening to the needs of my customers and team?
    iii. What steps can I take today to empower someone else in the dealership?
2. **Practical Strategies:**
    i. Schedule regular training sessions with sales staff to align them on financing and product knowledge.
    ii. Create a feedback loop to evaluate and improve the F&I process from customer and team perspectives.
    iii. Develop a simple checklist to ensure consistency in the Entry-Control-Execute process.

Example Checklist

1. **Entry:** Did I engage with the customer early?
2. **Control**: Have I aligned with the sales team and managed customer expectations?
3. **Execute:** Did I present solutions that genuinely meet the customer's needs?

Bridging Reflection to Action

Mastering the flow of Entry, Control, and Execute positions us for consistent success. Great leaders don't just focus on the present—they anticipate challenges and build systems to sustain excellence. In the next chapter, we'll explore how foresight and preparation can transform not just our results but the way we lead every day.

CHAPTER 15:
Structure and Organization

"Discipline is the bridge between goals and accomplishment."
— Jim Rohn

Success Begins with Structure

How you begin your day sets the tone for everything that follows. A structured morning routine doesn't just provide a strong foundation for your day—it sets the stage for success in your career and personal life. In the fast-paced world of automotive sales and service, a well-organized routine can distinguish top performers from those who struggle to keep up.

If you study the habits of high achievers across industries, you'll discover one consistent thread: A clearly defined morning routine. These individuals treat their mornings as sacred time—devoted to self-reflection, planning, and energizing their minds and bodies. In an industry known for its competitive intensity, preparation can mean the difference between leading the pack and falling behind.

The automotive industry is a complex ecosystem of manufacturing, sales, service, and innovation. Each sector requires meticulous organization, strategic thinking, and the ability to adapt. Tackling this complexity starts with a strong foundation: Your morning routine.

Understanding the Components of a Successful Morning Routine

1. Mindfulness and Reflection

Begin your day with mindfulness—whether through meditation, journaling, or quiet contemplation. This practice helps clear your mind, allowing you to focus on the day ahead. Writing down your goals, reflecting on challenges, or simply setting your intentions fosters mental clarity and emotional resilience—qualities that are critical in automotive leadership.

2. Physical Activity

Engaging in physical exercise energizes the body and sharpens the mind. Whether it's yoga, a morning walk, or a gym session, movement releases endorphins that elevate mood and boost cognitive performance. In a field where your energy level can directly impact your performance, this step is essential.

3. Nutrition

Start your day with a nutrient-rich breakfast. A balanced meal fuels your body for long hours and sustained focus. Proper nutrition reduces stress, enhances concentration, and keeps energy levels consistent throughout the day.

4. Planning and Prioritization

Every morning, identify your top priorities. Write down the most critical tasks, upcoming meetings, and long-term goals. By visualizing your day, you can approach your work with clarity and focus, reducing the feeling of overwhelm and increasing productivity.

5. Continuous Learning

In the ever-evolving automotive industry, staying informed is essential. Dedicate part of your morning to reading industry news, listening to relevant podcasts, or studying trends. This habit not only keeps you sharp but also positions you as a thought leader within your organization.

The Impact of Structure and Organization in the Automotive Industry

In the absence of structure, chaos often prevails. Organization is the backbone of both personal and professional success. Within the automotive industry, adopting a structured approach fosters innovation, efficiency, and resilience.

1. Organizational Structure

Successful dealerships thrive on clear organizational hierarchies. These structures enable smooth communication and efficient decision-making. Ensuring every team member understands their role and how it aligns with broader goals is vital to long-term success.

2. Lean Manufacturing Principles

Dealerships can benefit from lean manufacturing's focus on minimizing waste and maximizing efficiency. A well-organized showroom floor or F&I office leads to better productivity and profitability—both critical to maintaining a competitive edge.

3. Cross-Functional Collaboration

Encouraging collaboration among departments—sales, service, and finance—sparks innovation and improves problem-solving. Cross-functional teams ensure that everyone works toward shared objectives, enhancing customer satisfaction and dealership performance.

4. Data-Driven Decision Making

Dealerships that harness data to make decisions often outperform their competitors. Structured systems for collecting and analyzing data reveal trends in customer behavior, market demands, and operational inefficiencies. This intelligence helps leaders make informed decisions that drive growth and profitability.

Summary

Success in the automotive industry begins with structure—both in your personal habits and within the organization. A strong morning routine sets the tone for productivity, while a commitment to structured processes ensures efficiency and adaptability in an ever-changing market. By embracing these principles, individuals and teams can achieve long-term success and lead their dealerships to new heights.

Key Takeaways

1. A structured morning routine primes you for a successful day.
2. Mindfulness, exercise, nutrition, and planning are essential components of daily preparation.
3. Clear organizational frameworks foster communication, collaboration, and efficiency in the automotive sector.
4. Data-driven insights provide a competitive advantage in decision-making.
5. Cross-functional teamwork drives innovation and improves customer satisfaction.

Action Steps

For F&I Managers

1. Start your day by reviewing your schedule and prioritizing key tasks.
2. Ensure your office space is organized and customer-ready.
3. Regularly review industry trends and product updates to stay ahead of the curve.

For Dealership Teams

1. Collaborate on daily goals during team huddles or morning meetings.
2. Foster a culture of accountability by clearly defining each team member's responsibilities.
3. Adopt lean principles to streamline operations and improve customer experiences.

For Individual Professionals

1. Commit to a morning routine that includes mindfulness, exercise, and planning.
2. Identify one area of improvement—whether personal or professional—and dedicate time each morning to progress in that area.
3. Share industry insights with your team to foster knowledge-sharing and collaboration.

How to Apply This

In the F&I Office

1. **Streamline Workflows:** Ensure processes such as menu presentations are clear, consistent, and customer-focused.
2. **Organized Space:** Keep your workspace tidy to project professionalism and efficiency.
3. **Customer-Centric Approach:** Use structured strategies to build trust and address customer needs effectively.

Across the Dealership

1. **Foster Team Collaboration:** Implement systems that encourage teamwork across departments, such as joint strategy meetings.

2. **Leverage Technology:** Use CRM systems and data analytics to identify trends and improve customer service.
3. **Align Goals:** Ensure that all departments understand how their roles contribute to dealership success.

In Your Daily Practice

1. **Time Block Your Day:** Allocate specific times for key tasks to stay focused and efficient.
2. **Reflect Daily:** End each day by assessing what worked well and what could improve tomorrow.
3. **Stay Consistent:** Treat your routine as a non-negotiable part of your path to success.

Practical Tools for Success

1. **Morning Journal Template:** Use prompts to clarify goals, track progress, and set daily intentions.
2. **Priority Matrix:** Organize tasks by urgency and importance to focus your energy where it matters most.
3. **Accountability Partner:** Pair up with a colleague or mentor to keep each other on track with routines and goals.

Bridging Reflection to Action

Structure and organization are the lifeblood of leadership and success. By mastering your morning routine and embracing intentionality in all aspects of work, you create a ripple effect that inspires those around you. As you embrace structure and organization, you'll notice a transformation—not only in your mornings but also in your entire approach to work and life.

In Chapter 16, we'll build on these principles, exploring techniques that align with a structured approach to leadership. Together, these strategies will refine how you allocate resources, prioritize tasks, and lead with purpose.

CHAPTER 16:
Learn to Lead

"Leadership is not about being in charge. It's about taking care of those in your charge." — Simon Sinek

Leadership is a privilege—and with that privilege comes responsibility. Effective leadership doesn't just change the trajectory of your team; it shapes the entire organization's success. As F&I Managers, we're tasked not only with guiding our teams through complex transactions but also with fostering an environment where our team members feel valued and empowered. This chapter explores the essence of leadership through the lens of servant leadership, emphasizing the continuous journey of self-improvement and the responsibilities that come with it. To be great leaders, we must put our teams first, invest in their development, and lead with humility.

The Privilege of Leadership

In my years as an F&I Manager, I've come to understand one simple truth: Leadership isn't about power; it's about service. Our role as leaders is not to demand performance from our teams but to help them achieve success by creating an environment that nurtures their growth. Leadership is a privilege that comes with the responsibility of serving those we lead.

When I first stepped into a leadership role, I thought it was about telling people what to do and ensuring they met their targets. Over time, I realized that true leadership is about understanding the people on your team, serving them, and removing obstacles so they can succeed. Leadership isn't a position—it's a responsibility to guide, teach, and empower those around you.

Embracing the Servant Leadership Approach

The core of servant leadership is simple: You put others first. As an F&I Manager, your focus should be on serving your team members, helping them achieve their goals, and creating an atmosphere where they can thrive. This approach doesn't just improve the individual; it elevates the team and the entire organization.

For example, when I started prioritizing my team's needs and offering more support, I found that they were more motivated, engaged, and likely to meet their own goals. I made it my mission to understand each team member's strengths and weaknesses and worked alongside them to provide mentorship, encouragement, and training.

The Importance of Leadership in F&I

In the F&I department, we're often the last point of contact with customers, and how we lead our teams has a direct impact on customer satisfaction and dealership profitability. Leadership in F&I isn't just about directing—it's about motivating, empowering, and inspiring your team. True leaders focus on their people's growth and success, which, in turn, leads to better results for the entire department.

To truly lead in F&I, we must not only meet our own targets but also help our team members succeed. By fostering a culture of continuous learning, setting clear expectations, and giving consistent feedback, we drive results and build stronger, more resilient teams.

The 5 Levels of Leadership: A Servant Leader's Path

John Maxwell's *The 5 Levels of Leadership* changed the way I viewed my role as a leader. These five levels illustrate how leaders grow and influence others, progressing from simply holding a position to becoming a leader who inspires and empowers others to lead. As servant leaders, understanding these levels can help us better serve our teams and cultivate an environment where everyone can thrive.

1. **Position:** At the most basic level, leadership is granted based on position or title. While it's essential to establish authority, positional leadership is only the starting point. A servant leader must recognize that authority alone doesn't inspire loyalty or

commitment. To truly lead, you must earn the respect of your team through trust, service, and personal integrity.

2. **Permission:** This level is about building relationships and gaining trust. A servant leader listens actively, shows empathy, and values the input of team members. When team members feel heard and respected, they are more motivated and engaged in their work.

3. **Production:** At this level, leadership is defined by results. A servant leader produces results by helping their team succeed. The focus is not just on hitting targets but on coaching, supporting, and empowering team members to reach their goals. When leaders invest in their people, they produce a higher-performing team that is more accountable and motivated.

4. **People Development:** True leadership is about developing others. As a servant leader, mentoring and investing in your team's growth is crucial. By identifying individual strengths, providing skill-building opportunities, and offering recognition, you help your team grow personally and professionally. By ensuring your team's development, you create a culture of loyalty and long-term success.

5. **Pinnacle:** The pinnacle of leadership is when you become a leader who develops other leaders. A servant leader's ultimate goal is to create a legacy of leadership where each team member is empowered to lead themselves and others. This leadership level ensures the long-term health and success of the team and the organization.

Investing in Leadership Development

As F&I Managers, investing in leadership is critical—not just for ourselves but also for our teams. By prioritizing leadership development, we create a culture that thrives on growth, learning, and empowerment. Here's how you can invest in leadership within your department:

1. **Continuous Learning:** Encourage a culture of continuous learning by offering access to books, online courses, and industry seminars. A servant leader fosters an environment where team members constantly learn, improve, and stay updated with industry trends.

2. **Regular Feedback:** Create a culture where feedback is welcomed and constructive. One-on-one meetings provide a platform for team members to discuss their challenges,

successes, and goals. Regular feedback helps guide personal development and ensures the team stays on track.

3. **Leadership Workshops:** Offer workshops that focus on building leadership skills, communication, emotional intelligence, and conflict resolution. These workshops prepare team members for greater responsibilities, fostering a leadership mindset throughout the team.

4. **Mentorship Programs:** Create mentorship initiatives where experienced team members guide newer ones. A servant leader's role is to nurture and guide others, helping them develop their leadership potential. Mentorship builds confidence, transfers knowledge, and creates a stronger, more cohesive team.

5. **Celebrate Achievements:** Recognize and celebrate the achievements of your team. Acknowledging hard work, growth, and success boosts morale and reinforces the value of collective achievement. Servant leaders celebrate the wins of their team, not just their own.

Summary

Leadership is about serving others, not being served. As F&I Managers, we are responsible for leading with humility, empowering our teams, and developing future leaders. By focusing on the growth and development of our teams, we create stronger, more motivated employees who will, in turn, lead the way to organizational success. Leadership is an ongoing journey, and embracing servant leadership principles ensures that we remain committed to our personal growth and the success of those we lead.

Key Takeaways

1. Servant leadership is about prioritizing the development and well-being of others.
2. Leadership is a privilege and should be exercised with humility and integrity.
3. Empowering your team and fostering their growth leads to long-term success.
4. John Maxwell's *5 Levels of Leadership* offer a roadmap for evolving as a leader.
5. Investing in continuous learning, feedback, and mentorship helps cultivate a strong, engaged team.

Action Steps

For F&I Managers

1. Embrace a servant leadership mindset by focusing on the needs of your team.
2. Create an environment of open communication and continuous feedback.
3. Invest in your team's growth by offering training, mentorship, and development opportunities.

For Dealership Teams

1. Work together to foster a culture of trust, collaboration, and mutual respect.
2. Support each other's growth and offer constructive feedback to help each other improve.
3. Encourage team members to step into leadership roles and empower them to develop their leadership skills.

For Individual Professionals

1. Commit to lifelong learning by seeking opportunities for growth and development.
2. Be proactive in offering support and guidance to your peers and juniors.
3. Focus on building strong, authentic relationships with your colleagues and customers.

How to Apply This

In the F&I Office

1. Focus on serving your team's needs, whether it's through training, guidance, or personal support.
2. Use your position to coach, mentor, and empower others to step into leadership roles.

Across the Dealership

1. Encourage a culture where leadership development is seen as a team effort, and everyone is responsible for contributing to the team's success.
2. Align team goals with a shared vision of growth, accountability, and customer service.

In Your Daily Practice

1. Start each day with the mindset of serving others, whether it's your team, customers, or colleagues.
2. Reflect on how you can serve and support those around you to help them grow and succeed.

Practical Tools for Success

1. **Leadership Development Plan**: Create a personalized plan for your own leadership growth, identifying areas for improvement and opportunities for learning.
2. **Team Development Tracker**: Develop a system for tracking the growth and achievements of your team, celebrating milestones along the way.
3. **Mentorship Map**: Establish a mentorship framework to guide your team members toward leadership roles.

Reflection Questions

Personal Practice

1. How can I better serve the needs of my team to help them grow and succeed?

Resilience

2. How do I stay humble and open to feedback while continuously improving my leadership abilities?

Teamwork

3. How can I foster an environment where collaboration and leadership are encouraged across all levels of the team?

Growth

4. What specific steps can I take to continue developing my own leadership skills and those of my team?

Bridging Reflection to Action

In the next chapter, we'll discuss how to apply these principles during times of challenge or change, ensuring that leadership remains strong even in tough circumstances. By committing to lifelong growth and development, you will continue to lead with purpose, integrity, and success.

CHAPTER 17:

The Pursuit of Personal Development

"The pursuit of personal development is not just a personal choice; it is a professional necessity." — Unknown

Personal development isn't optional—it's a **must**. You can't just sit back and expect to succeed in this industry without **constantly leveling up**. As F&I Managers, we are the cornerstone of the dealership; the better we are, the better our teams and the entire organization become. This chapter is here to remind you that personal growth is a **continuous journey**—one that makes you better, **not just for you** but for your team and your customers. It's about becoming a leader who **serves and empowers** others—because when they grow, you grow.

I've been committed to personal development for as long as I can remember and trust me when I say that it has **transformed everything**. It gave me the tools to navigate the challenges of the automotive world with confidence, resilience, and a much clearer vision of what I needed to do to get ahead. Once I decided to **focus on improving myself daily**, everything else fell into place. Doors opened. Opportunities appeared. And it all started with **deciding** to work on myself, personally and professionally, every single day.

The Importance of Personal Development in F&I

As an F&I Manager, you're sitting at the crossroads of customer service, sales, and compliance. If you can't adapt, communicate effectively, or deliver world-class service, you won't last long. Personal development is what helps us **sharpen those skills** and elevate our ability to **serve** the customer, our team, and our business. The better we get at managing ourselves and growing our skills, the more successful we will be.

Here's the deal: If you want to be great at what you do, you need to follow the greats. Look around at the leaders in the automotive industry—they're the ones pushing boundaries, driving change, and making a real impact. By learning from their stories, strategies, and mindsets, you'll be able to tap into the same **drive and ambition** that propels them forward.

1. **Study Successful Leaders:** Don't wait for someone to hand you the keys to success. Take control of your learning. Read books, listen to podcasts, and watch interviews with leaders like Elon Musk, Ali Reda, Brian Benstock, and Jim Farley. These guys aren't just successful—they've **transformed industries**. Learn from their leadership style, their innovation, and their commitment to excellence. Those lessons are priceless.

2. **Attend Industry Conferences:** Get out there and **connect**. Going to industry conferences isn't just about hearing the latest trends—it's about surrounding yourself with people who inspire you, challenge your thinking, and offer new ideas. Networking with people who are already excelling in their field can give you the push you need to **step up your game**.

3. **Find a Mentor:** Mentorship is huge. Find someone who's been there, done that, and has the scars to prove it. A mentor can **accelerate** your growth. They'll help you avoid common mistakes and pass on their wisdom, showing you how to be **a better leader** and serve your team. You don't have to do it all alone; let someone guide you.

4. **Join Professional Networks:** There's strength in numbers. By joining professional organizations or networks, you surround yourself with people who are just as hungry as you are. You can **learn from others**, share experiences, and hold each other accountable. Get in these circles—they'll help you grow, and you'll get a chance to serve others along the way.

Habits of Superachievers

Superachievers don't just get lucky—they build their success day by day. If you want to be a super achiever, you need to adopt these habits. Here's the thing: **Superachievers aren't perfect**, but they show up, they commit, and they **always serve** those around them through their work ethic and attitude.

1. **Set Clear Goals**: You can't hit a target if you don't know where it is. Write down your goals. Get clear on them. If you're not looking at them every day, you're doing it wrong. Set an action plan to go after them. **A goal without a plan is just a wish**.

2. **Take Responsibility**: Own it. If something goes wrong, take accountability. Don't play the victim—**learn from mistakes** and **move forward**. That's how you build trust and serve your team effectively.

3. **Discipline Yourself**: Discipline gets easier when you're aligned with your purpose. **When you know why you're doing it,** you won't need external motivation. You'll stick to your routine because you know it leads to growth and service.

4. **Maintain a Healthy Lifestyle**: Success starts with **your health**. You can't serve anyone else if you're not feeling your best. Take care of your body—it's your biggest asset.

5. **Stick to Your Non-Negotiables**: Establish what's **non-negotiable** in your life—things like your morning routine, your work ethic, your time with family, etc. Stick to them. The best leaders do.

6. **Be Obsessed with Self-Development**: Superachievers are **relentless** in their pursuit of growth. They never stop learning. They are always working to **better themselves**.

7. **Embrace New Ideas**: They're open to new methods, ideas, and opportunities. They **never stop innovating**.

8. **Get a Mentor**: They don't shy away from asking for help. They know the value of mentorship in **serving others**.

9. **Aim Higher**: Superachievers always **push** themselves to the next level.

10. **Read Every Day**: Reading isn't just for fun; it's for **personal growth**. Successful people dedicate time every day to feed their minds.

11. **Manage Time Like a Pro**: Time is the **most valuable resource**. Superachievers plan their days, prioritize tasks, and **focus**. They know that better time management leads to higher income.

12. **Take Risks**: You can't grow without taking risks. Failure is **inevitable**, but so is success if you **embrace** it.

13. **Stay Confident**: Superachievers are confident in their ability to overcome setbacks. They **view challenges as learning opportunities**, not roadblocks.

14. **Never Quit**: The winners keep going, no matter what gets in their way.

15. **Always Find a Way to Win**: If you're not winning, you're learning. Winners don't give up.

16. **Relentless in Pursuit**: They're obsessed with **winning**. They focus on what's important and block out distractions.

17. **Do What You Love**: When you love what you do, work doesn't feel like work. Find your purpose and **serve others** through your passion.

The Journey is Ongoing

Personal development doesn't have an endpoint. Once you think you've arrived, that's when you stop growing. Life is about **constant evolution**, and the automotive industry is no different. Every new challenge is an opportunity to grow, serve, and improve.

The key is making small, **incremental improvements** every day. Embrace **kaizen** or continuous improvement. If you can make just a little progress each day, you'll look back a year from now and be amazed at how far you've come.

Practical Steps to Apply Personal Development

1. **Set Personal Goals:** Develop SMART goals—specific, measurable, achievable, relevant, and time-bound. Whether it's improving your sales techniques or your ability to manage teams, make sure your goals are clear and actionable.
2. **Create a Learning Plan:** Your learning plan should include books, courses, and activities that help you grow. Ensure your learning aligns with your long-term growth and development so you're always moving forward.
3. **Reflect and Assess:** Take time to regularly assess your progress. Reflect on what you've learned, what worked, and where you still have room for improvement. **Self-reflection is key** to personal and leadership development.
4. **Embrace Challenges:** Challenges are **growth opportunities**. Take them head-on and **view each challenge** as a way to build resilience, knowledge, and leadership skills.

Summary

Personal development is a continuous journey. The more we focus on improving ourselves, the more we can serve our teams, customers, and organizations. Small, consistent improvements, paired with a commitment to learning from those who've come before us, will transform our careers. But it's not just about personal success—it's about creating an environment where our teams grow with us. Serve others, grow yourself, and build the future you want to see.

Key Takeaways

1. Personal development is essential for both personal success and **serving others**.
2. **Servant leadership** isn't just about guiding others; it's about growing alongside them.
3. Learn from great leaders, embrace continuous improvement, and push yourself to grow.
4. Set **SMART goals** and create a structured development plan.
5. **Embrace challenges** as opportunities for growth and service.

Action Steps

For F&I Managers

1. **Set SMART goals** and keep them front and center.
2. Lead by **serving your team**—prioritize their development.
3. Regularly **reflect on your progress** and adapt your strategy as needed.

For Dealership Teams

1. Foster a culture of **learning** and **continuous growth**.
2. Share your knowledge and experiences—help each other **grow**.
3. **Support** each other's development by setting up mentorship programs.

For Individual Professionals

1. **Invest in your own development**—seek out mentorship, learning opportunities, and growth.
2. **Reflect daily** on your progress and take responsibility for your growth.
3. **Serve others** through your actions and share what you've learned.

How to Apply This

In the F&I Office

1. Focus on developing yourself and your team, always **leading with a servant mindset**.
2. Invest time in **continuous learning** and adapt strategies to meet evolving industry demands.

Across the Dealership

1. Create an environment that prioritizes growth for all team members.
2. Encourage mentorship and shared learning across departments to **serve and uplift** others.

In Your Daily Practice

1. Commit to **small, daily improvements**—take action to serve yourself and your team each day.

Practical Tools for Success

1. **Goal-Setting Worksheet**: A tool to help you break down goals into actionable steps.
2. **Learning Plan Template**: A structured roadmap to guide your continuous personal development.
3. **Reflection Journal**: A tool for tracking progress, identifying strengths, and addressing areas for improvement.

Reflection Questions

Personal Practice

1. How am I serving my team through my personal development journey?

Resilience

2. How do I respond to challenges, and how can I frame them as growth opportunities?

Teamwork

3. What can I do to help serve my team and inspire their growth?

Growth

4. What are my next steps for continuous development?

Bridging Reflection to Action

In the next chapter, we'll explore how to maintain momentum and continue growing during times of **stress** and **change**. Embracing **servant leadership** ensures we stay focused on growth for ourselves and those we lead.

CHAPTER 18:
Embrace Change

"If you continue to do what you're doing right now, you will continue to get the same results." — Unknown

Introduction

If you keep doing what you're doing now, you'll keep getting the same results. That statement is so simple, yet it's one of the most profound truths about growth. You're reading this book because you want more— more success, more opportunities, and more personal and professional fulfillment. Here's the hard truth: To get there, you must **embrace change**.

Being an F&I Manager isn't just a job; it's a **privilege**. But with that privilege comes a **responsibility**—to yourself, your team, your dealership, and your customers. Change is where **growth begins**. It's uncomfortable, yes, but it's also the key to innovation, improvement, and success. By embracing change, you can transform your career and the lives of those you serve.

The Importance of Embracing Change in F&I

Over the years, I've worked with thousands of dealerships and built incredible partnerships with some of the most prestigious OEMs in the industry. One thing I've learned is this: The dealerships that **embrace change** thrive, while those that resist it stagnate. The automotive landscape is always evolving. **Customer preferences shift, technology advances, and competitors emerge.** If we aren't willing to adapt, we'll fall behind.

It's easy to get comfortable with what we know—the systems, the strategies, the processes that have worked in the past. But being comfortable often leads to being complacent. And complacency? That's the enemy of growth. To lead your team and dealership to success, you must stay open to new ideas, approaches, and possibilities. You must lead the charge when it comes to embracing change.

A Lesson in Adaptability: *Who Moved My Cheese?*

Years ago, I read a book that completely changed my perspective on change: *Who Moved My Cheese?* by Spencer Johnson. It's a story about two mice, Sniff and Scurry, and two little people, Hem and Haw. Their cheese—a metaphor for success, security, or comfort—gets moved. The way they respond to this change determines their future.

1. Sniff and Scurry don't waste time mourning the loss of their cheese. They **adapt quickly**, set out to find new cheese, and ultimately thrive.
2. Hem and Haw, on the other hand, resist change. They cling to what they know, hoping things will go back to how they were. **They stay stuck** while others move forward.

Eventually, Haw realizes that change is necessary. He steps out of his comfort zone, embraces the unknown, and finds new opportunities. That story hit me like a ton of bricks. It made me realize that success isn't about staying comfortable but **embracing discomfort** and chasing growth.

As an F&I Manager, you need to adopt the mindset of Sniff and Scurry. Be proactive. Be adaptable. Embrace change as an opportunity, not a threat. When you do, you'll discover new ways to serve your customers, empower your team, and elevate your dealership.

How Change Makes You a Better Leader

Change isn't just about personal growth—it's about **serving others**. When you embrace change, you set the tone for your team. You show them that adaptability isn't optional; it's a requirement for success. As a leader, your job is to help your team navigate change, stay open to new ideas, and remain resilient through challenges.

Think about how you engage with your customers. Are you using the latest tools to improve their experience? Are you offering financing options that align with today's consumer needs? **Innovation isn't just about staying competitive—it's about serving your customers better.**

The same goes for your team. When you encourage change, you create a **culture of growth and collaboration**. Invite your team to share ideas, try new approaches, and learn from their failures. Remind them that failure isn't the opposite of success—it's part of the process. A team that feels empowered to adapt and innovate will always outperform one that clings to outdated methods.

Practical Ways to Embrace Change

Change doesn't have to be overwhelming. Start small. Take one step at a time, and soon it will become second nature. Here are some practical ways to make change part of your routine:

1. **Experiment Daily:** Try something new every day, whether it's a new tool, technique, or approach to problem-solving. The more you practice adapting, the more comfortable you'll become with change.
2. **Welcome Feedback:** Feedback is one of the most valuable tools for growth. Ask your team, your peers, and even your customers how you can improve. Listen closely and act on what you learn.
3. **Encourage Innovation:** Create an environment where your team feels safe to share ideas and try new things. Celebrate their successes and use failures as learning opportunities.
4. **Stay Educated:** The automotive industry is always changing. Stay ahead by reading books, attending conferences, and connecting with industry leaders. The more you know, the better you'll lead.

Summary

Change isn't just inevitable—it's essential. It separates leaders from followers, innovators from imitators, and thriving dealerships from stagnant ones. When you embrace change, you position yourself, your team, and your dealership for long-term success. Remember, growth doesn't happen without discomfort. Step out of your comfort zone, lead with courage, and inspire those around you to do the same.

Key Takeaways

1. **Change is a catalyst for growth.** Without it, you can't evolve personally or professionally.
2. **Lead by example.** When you embrace change, you encourage your team to follow.
3. **Innovation drives success.** Stay open to new tools, technologies, and strategies.

4. **Discomfort equals growth.** Growth happens when you step outside of your comfort zone.
5. **Empower your team.** Create a culture where change and experimentation are embraced.

Action Steps

For F&I Managers

1. Identify one area in your work where you can embrace change today—whether it's trying a new technology or rethinking your customer approach.
2. Host regular team meetings to discuss new ideas and strategies for adapting to industry changes.

For Dealership Teams

1. Create a shared space for innovation where team members can share ideas, feedback, and suggestions for improvement.
2. Celebrate team members who take risks and embrace change, even if the results aren't perfect.

For Individual Professionals

1. Commit to personal growth by reading books, attending seminars, or seeking mentorship.
2. Practice stepping out of your comfort zone daily—it's where real growth happens.

How to Apply This

In the F&I Office

1. Introduce new technologies or processes that enhance the customer experience.
2. Lead training sessions focused on helping your team adapt to new tools or methods.

Across the Dealership

1. Foster collaboration between departments to align everyone around the need for change.
2. Share success stories of how embracing change has led to better results.

In Your Daily Practice

1. Start each day with a willingness to try something new and embrace discomfort as part of the growth process.

Practical Tools for Success

1. **Change Log**: Track the changes you've implemented and the results they've achieved.
2. **Feedback Checklist**: Use this to collect and act on feedback from your team and customers.
3. **Innovation Journal**: Document new ideas, lessons learned, and next steps for improvement.

Reflection Questions

Personal Practice

1. How can I embrace change in a way that benefits my team and customers?

Resilience

2. What's my typical response to change, and how can I shift it to be more positive?

Teamwork

3. How can I help my team feel more comfortable with change and encourage innovation?

Growth

4. What's one area in my professional life where I need to step out of my comfort zone?

Bridging Reflection to Action

Change isn't just something you deal with—it's something you embrace to grow stronger, smarter, and more successful. In the next chapter, we'll explore how to turn the momentum from embracing change into sustained success. Let's keep moving forward, ready to lead with courage and purpose.

CHAPTER 19:
Take Action

"Taking action is the bridge that connects dreams with reality." —
Grant Cardone

The gap between inspiration and execution is staggering. Think about it—there are countless incredible ideas out there, but most never materialize. Why? Because people fail to take action. They attend sales seminars, join personal development groups, and soak up valuable insights, only to return to their old habits without implementing a single change.

DO NOT be that person. You are better than that. You have the power to rise above mediocrity and achieve greatness. You deserve more—more success, more fulfillment, and more income to provide for your family and serve your community. The key to unlocking all of this lies in one fundamental principle: **Taking action**.

Action is what separates the dreamers from the achievers. It's not enough to be inspired—you must execute. Taking action isn't just about bettering yourself; it's about using your growth to **serve others** and make an impact. This is where true leadership begins.

The Power of Taking Massive Action

If you want to turn your ideas into results, you must take **massive action**. This means diving in fully, committing to the process, and embracing the challenges that come with meaningful change.

Grant Cardone's book, *The 10X Rule*, transformed how I view action. His message is simple yet profound: **Those who do more will get more.** Taking 10X action means going beyond ordinary effort. It's about **pushing harder**, aiming higher, and striving for extraordinary results. The key lesson? **Stop waiting for opportunities and start creating them.**

When you take massive action, you aren't just working toward your goals—you're creating ripples of impact that affect your team, dealership, and customers. Action fuels service. It's how you lead by example, inspire others, and show what's possible.

Overcoming the Challenges of Action

Let's be real: Taking action isn't always easy. It requires **discipline, consistency, and resilience**. There will be days when you're exhausted or discouraged. But this is where leaders rise above the rest.

Adopt this mindset:

Don't go to bed when you're tired—go to bed when you're done.

This principle will instill in you the tenacity required to overcome obstacles. Success isn't about waiting for perfect conditions; it's about making progress, even when it feels messy or uncomfortable. Every step forward, no matter how small, is a step closer to achieving your goals.

As a servant leader, your ability to push through challenges isn't just for you—it's for those who rely on you. When you keep moving forward, you inspire your team to do the same. You show them that action isn't about perfection but perseverance.

Stories of Success Through Action

The people we admire most—the ones who've achieved massive success—didn't get there by waiting for the perfect moment. They got there because they refused to let inaction hold them back. They faced failures, learned hard lessons, and kept moving forward.

What sets these individuals apart is their commitment to action. They didn't wait for permission or let fear stop them. They took bold steps and embraced every challenge as an opportunity to grow. Their journeys remind us that action isn't about being fearless; it's about **acting despite fear** and using each failure as a stepping stone toward success.

How F&I Managers Can Take Action

As an F&I Manager, you have daily opportunities to put this principle into practice. Whether it's refining your sales techniques, improving the customer experience, or fostering collaboration within your team, every action you take contributes to your dealership's success. The key is to prioritize **action over perfection**.

Stop waiting for the perfect time to start. There is no perfect time. Take the first step—no matter how small—and build momentum. Each small action compounds into bigger results. As you take action, remember that your efforts aren't just about hitting your own goals; they're about **serving your team and your customers**, creating better experiences for everyone involved.

Creating a Culture of Action

Taking action isn't just about personal growth—it's about creating a culture where everyone feels empowered to take initiative and make an impact. Here's how you can foster a culture of action within your dealership:

1. **Encourage Initiative**: Empower your team to take ownership of their ideas and responsibilities. Let them know their contributions matter.
2. **Celebrate Effort, Not Just Results**: Recognize team members who step up, even if the results aren't perfect. This fosters a mindset of experimentation and growth.
3. **Lead by Example**: Show your team what it looks like to take bold, consistent action. When they see you leading with energy and determination, they'll follow your lead.

As a servant leader, your job is to create an environment where your team feels supported and inspired to take action. When you empower others to act, you build collective momentum that benefits everyone.

Practical Steps to Take Action

Taking action doesn't have to be overwhelming. Start small and build from there. Here are some practical steps you can implement today:

1. **Set Clear Goals**: Define what you want to achieve and break it down into actionable steps. Make sure your goals are SMART—specific, measurable, achievable, relevant, and time-bound.
2. **Take the First Step**: Don't wait for ideal conditions. Take action today, no matter how small.
3. **Commit to Consistency**: Build a daily habit of taking action. Small, consistent efforts lead to big results over time.
4. **Learn from Mistakes**: View setbacks as opportunities for growth, not reasons to stop. Every failure is a lesson.
5. **Measure Your Progress**: Regularly track your efforts and results to stay motivated and focused.

Summary

Action is the bridge between dreams and reality. Without it, even the best ideas go nowhere. By embracing the mindset of massive action, you unlock the potential to create meaningful change for yourself, your team, and your dealership. **Don't let your ideas stay ideas.** Take action, inspire those around you, and watch your efforts lead to success beyond what you thought possible.

Key Takeaways

1. **Action is the key to success.** Ideas without action are meaningless.
2. **Massive action leads to extraordinary results.** Push beyond average efforts to achieve greatness.
3. Prioritize progress over perfection. Start messy, but start now.
4. **Action inspires others.** As a servant leader, your efforts create a culture of growth and initiative.
5. **Consistency wins.** Daily habits of disciplined action lead to long-term success.

Action Steps

For F&I Managers:

1. Identify one specific area where you can take immediate action, such as improving customer engagement or refining sales strategies.
2. Set a goal for your team and take the first step toward achieving it today.

For Dealership Teams

1. Host brainstorming sessions where team members can share actionable ideas for improvement.
2. Recognize and reward team members who take initiative, even if the results aren't perfect.

For Individual Professionals

1. Write down one goal you've been avoiding and commit to acting on it today.
2. Find an accountability partner to keep you motivated and focused.

How to Apply This

In the F&I Office

1. Experiment with new approaches to customer engagement or financing strategies.
2. Lead by example, showing your team what it looks like to take bold action.

Across the Dealership

1. Encourage cross-department collaboration to share ideas and best practices.
2. Celebrate team successes that result from bold actions and innovation.

In Your Daily Practice

1. Start each day with an action plan. Write down three things you'll accomplish before the day ends.

Practical Tools for Success

1. **Action Tracker**: A simple tool to track your progress toward specific goals.
2. **Daily Momentum Checklist**: A daily list of three key actions to keep you consistent.
3. **Recognition Board**: A way to celebrate team members who take the initiative and drive results.

Reflection Questions

Personal Practice

1. What's one area in my life where I need to stop planning and start doing?

Resilience

2. How do I handle setbacks, and how can I reframe them as opportunities for growth?

Teamwork

3. How can I inspire my team to take bold action and prioritize progress over perfection?

Growth

4. What's one small step I can take today to build momentum toward a larger goal?

Bridging Reflection to Action

Taking action isn't just a step—it's a lifestyle. It's about showing up, pushing forward, and leading by example every single day. In the next chapter, we'll explore how to sustain this momentum and turn action into long-term success. **Remember: you deserve it all—now go out and claim it.**

CHAPTER 20:

Transact the Way Your Customer Wants To

"Customers don't want to be sold—they want to buy on their terms." — Adam Marburger

Let me start with something I've wanted to say for a long time: **Never get upset with your sales consultant because a customer is paying cash for their vehicle.** I've seen this play out far too often—F&I Managers getting frustrated over how a customer chooses to pay. Let's be clear: **Not all deals will be financing deals, and that's perfectly fine.** Our job is to treat every transaction with respect and professionalism, regardless of the payment method.

Cash, finance, or lease—each method is simply a way for customers to pay for their vehicle. **Every transaction is an opportunity to serve.** Servant leadership means respecting the preferences of your customers, meeting them where they are, and delivering a seamless and empowering experience. The customer's choices should never feel like a problem; they should feel like the priority.

The Importance of Respecting Customer Preferences

Customers today expect flexibility, and it's our responsibility to adapt to their preferences. The world of automotive retailing has changed dramatically. Digital retailing is no longer just a buzzword; it's the reality of how many customers want to shop. Companies like AutoFI offer tools that make the transaction process seamless, giving their customers the freedom to engage in a way that works best for them.

Here's the truth: **Customers want to buy F&I products; they just don't want to feel like they're being sold something.** When we respect their preferences and create an experience that feels transparent and empowering, they're more likely to trust us and engage with what we offer.

How F&I Managers Can Lead Through Change

Adapting to customer preferences isn't just about staying relevant; it's about **serving your customers better** and creating a culture of excellence within your dealership. As leaders, we set the tone for how our teams approach change and innovation. Here's how you can lead by example:

1. Understand Customer Preferences

Take the time to truly understand how your customers want to interact with you. Do they prefer a streamlined online process, face-to-face interactions, or a mix of both? By tailoring your approach to meet their needs, you'll make their experience smoother and more enjoyable.

2. Embrace Technology

Equip yourself and your team with tools that make digital retailing easy and effective. Platforms like AutoFI simplify the online and in store process. Familiarize your team with these technologies and invest in training so they can confidently guide customers through any scenario.

3. Provide Transparency

Transparency builds trust. Customers appreciate clear, straightforward pricing and product options. When they feel informed and in control, they're more likely to invest in the solutions you provide. Transparency isn't just a tactic—it's the foundation of trust and long-term relationships.

4. Be Adaptable

The automotive industry is constantly evolving, and customer expectations are changing with it. As a leader, staying adaptable and open to new ideas is essential. Adaptability isn't just about following trends; it's about leading your team through them with confidence and clarity.

5. Foster a Customer-Centric Culture

Create a culture where your team puts the customer first in every interaction. When they prioritize the customer's preferences, you'll see higher satisfaction rates, repeat business, and more positive referrals.

Servant leadership means making the customer the focus of everything you do.

Breaking Down Silos: Sales and F&I Collaboration

A seamless customer experience requires teamwork, especially between sales and F&I. Too often, conflict arises when sales and F&I don't align, especially over issues like cash payments. This siloed approach does nothing but harm the customer's experience.

When sales and F&I teams work together to prioritize the customer, the result is a unified approach that makes the customer feel valued at every step. Breaking down silos fosters collaboration, which leads to smoother transactions and stronger customer relationships.

Creating a Win-Win Environment

When you let customers transact the way they want, everyone wins. Research consistently shows that when customers feel in control and have easy-to-understand options, they're more likely to select F&I products. This reduces pressure on your team and increases engagement from your customers.

It's not about selling. Instead, it's about **facilitating a purchase process that aligns with your customer's needs.** By adopting this mindset, you position yourself and your dealership as trusted partners in the buying process, building trust and loyalty in the long term.

Practical Steps to Transact the Way Customers Want

To put this into action, here are some practical steps to align your dealership with modern customer preferences:

1. **Listen to Your Customers:** Regularly collect feedback to understand how your customers prefer to transact. Use this insight to refine your approach and meet their expectations.
2. **Leverage Digital Tools:** Invest in digital platforms like AutoFI that make the transactions seamless. Ensure your team is comfortable using these tools to guide customers effectively.
3. **Train Your Team:** Provide ongoing training so your staff can confidently handle both digital and in-person transactions.

Empower them to navigate changes and offer personalized service in every scenario.

4. **Simplify the Process:** Make the transaction process as straightforward as possible. Provide clear options and focus on reducing friction at every step.

5. **Celebrate Successes:** Recognize team members who adapt to customer preferences and excel in delivering exceptional service. Share their achievements to inspire others.

Summary

The future of automotive retailing is customer-driven. Success in this industry comes down to one simple principle: **Respect how your customers want to transact.** Whether they choose to pay cash, finance, lease, or complete their purchase online, the key is to meet them where they are.

As F&I Managers, we have the privilege and responsibility to create experiences that empower our customers and build trust. By embracing change and leading with a servant's heart, we can transform our dealerships into leaders in the industry. **Don't just adapt to the future—lead it.**

Key Takeaways

1. **Respect customer preferences.** Treat every payment method—cash, finance, or lease—with equal professionalism.
2. **Embrace digital retailing.** Customers increasingly value seamless online transactions.
3. **Transparency builds trust.** Be clear and honest about pricing and product options.
4. **Adaptability is essential.** Stay informed about trends and lead your team through change.
5. **A customer-first culture wins.** Prioritizing customer needs leads to higher satisfaction and loyalty.

Action Steps

For F&I Managers

1. Review your transaction process and identify areas where you can better align with customer preferences.

2. Host a team meeting to discuss strategies for improving collaboration between sales and F&I.

For Dealership Teams

1. Invest in training that equips staff to handle both digital and in-person transactions effectively.
2. Collect customer feedback and use it to refine your approach.

For Individual Professionals

1. Learn about the latest trends in digital retailing and explore tools like AutoFI.
2. Focus on providing clear, transparent options for customers to build trust and engagement.

How to Apply This

In the F&I Office

1. Use digital platforms to create a seamless, stress-free experience for customers.
2. Ensure every transaction is treated with respect and professionalism, no matter the payment method.

Across the Dealership

1. Foster collaboration between departments to create a unified, customer-first approach.
2. Celebrate team members who excel at adapting to customer needs.

In Your Daily Practice

1. Start each day by reflecting on how you can better serve your customers and team.
2. Commit to embracing change and leading by example.

Practical Tools for Success

1. **Customer Preference Tracker**: Log and analyze customer feedback on transaction preferences.
2. **Digital Retailing Playbook**: A guide for using online tools to streamline the buying process.
3. **Team Training Calendar**: Schedule ongoing training sessions on digital and in-person transactions.

Reflection Questions

Personal Practice

1. How can I better respect and adapt to my customers' transaction preferences?

Resilience

2. How can I lead my team through changes in the automotive industry with confidence?

Teamwork

3. What steps can I take to foster a culture that prioritizes customer needs above all else?

Growth

4. How can I embrace digital tools to enhance both customer experience and team efficiency?

Bridging Reflection to Action

The future of automotive transactions is here. It's digital, customer-driven, and constantly evolving. By embracing these changes and leading with a servant's heart, you can transform your dealership into a leader in the industry. **Remember: Customers want to buy on their terms; your job is to make that possible.** Let's lead the way into the future.

CHAPTER 21:
Stop Obsessing Over PVR

"Focus on serving the customer, and the numbers will take care of themselves." — Adam Marburger

As I reflect on my journey in the automotive finance industry, one pivotal moment stands out: **The day I decided to stop obsessing over my profit Per Vehicle Retailed (PVR).** For too long, I let this number dictate my mood, my approach, and how I interacted with customers. Every day, I found myself checking it like a stock ticker, allowing its fluctuations to consume me.

Then everything changed. I made a simple yet profound decision: **To stop focusing on the number and start focusing on the customer.** That shift in mindset transformed my career, my relationships with customers, and my ability to lead effectively.

Servant leadership begins with putting the customer first, not the metrics. By focusing on **how we can serve others**, we achieve results that far exceed what chasing numbers can deliver. This chapter is about adopting that mindset and transforming the way you approach your role in F&I.

The Turning Point: Focusing on the Customer

Instead of obsessing over my daily PVR, I started setting **monthly goals** based on my previous performance. This gave me clarity and direction without the stress of daily fluctuations. It allowed me to put on blinders and concentrate solely on the **customer in front of me.**

When I stopped worrying about the number and started focusing on **serving the client**, I found that I could create a much higher level of service. My primary goal became clear: **To serve the customer and create a positive experience from the very first interaction.**

This change didn't just benefit my customers—it benefited me. It allowed me to engage with customers earlier in the process, take control of the deal more effectively, and set a positive tone for the entire transaction.

Here's the lesson: When you prioritize the relationship over the transaction, the numbers will naturally follow. Your role as an F&I Manager isn't just about closing deals; it's about building trust, solving problems, and creating value for every customer you interact with.

Why Obsessing Over Metrics Can Hurt Your Performance

It's easy to get caught up in the whirlwind of metrics. Numbers are tangible and feel like a concrete way to measure your performance. But when you let numbers like PVR dictate your every move, it's easy to lose sight of what truly matters: The **human element of your work.**

Constantly evaluating yourself against a single metric can lead to:

1. **Self-Doubt**: When the numbers aren't where you want them to be, it's easy to feel like you're failing.
2. **Tunnel Vision**: You focus so much on the metric that you miss opportunities to genuinely connect with customers.
3. **Missed Opportunities**: By focusing solely on the transaction, you fail to create long-term value and trust.

To thrive as an F&I Manager, you need to shift your perspective. Your success isn't defined by a daily number; it's defined by the value you bring to your customers and your team.

Skills Every F&I Manager Should Master

If you want to excel without obsessing over PVR, here are some key areas to focus on:

1. Master Your Product Knowledge

Knowing your products inside and out is the foundation of effective F&I management. Customers trust professionals who are confident and knowledgeable. When you understand every detail of the products you offer, you can tailor solutions that meet their needs.

2. Perfect Your Presentation Skills

How you present your products matters just as much as the products themselves. Develop a presentation style that feels authentic, confident, and customer-focused. When customers feel your enthusiasm and belief in what you're offering, they're more likely to engage.

3. Identify Customer Personality Types

Every customer is different. Some are analytical and want the data, while others make decisions based on relationships or emotions. Learn to identify personality types quickly and adapt your approach to match their style.

4. Tailor Your Approach

Once you understand a customer's personality type, customize your pitch. For example:

1. An analytical customer might appreciate detailed cost-benefit analyses.
2. A relationship-oriented customer might respond better to personal stories or testimonials.

This level of personalization not only enhances the customer's experience but also increases your chances of success.

The Process is the Key to Success

By honing these skills, you'll be able to deliver results without the stress of obsessing over daily metrics. The process is straightforward:

1. Serve the customer first.
2. Follow the steps consistently.
3. Let the numbers speak for themselves.

When you focus on creating value for the customer, everything else falls into place. **Remember: The highest PVRs belong to those who prioritize relationships, not transactions.**

Adopting a Servant Leadership Mindset

At its core, servant leadership is about prioritizing the needs of others. In the context of F&I, this means:

1. **Listening** to your customers to understand their needs and concerns.

2. **Providing solutions** that genuinely benefit them.
3. Focusing on long-term relationships over short-term gains.

When you lead with a servant's heart, your customers will notice. They'll feel valued, respected, and empowered, and that trust will translate into better outcomes for everyone involved.

Practical Steps to Stop Obsessing Over PVR

Here's how you can shift your focus and adopt a more customer-centric approach:

1. **Set Monthly Goals:** Replace daily PVR checks with monthly performance goals. This reduces anxiety and keeps you focused on the bigger picture.
2. **Engage Early:** Build relationships with customers early in the process. The sooner you connect, the more trust you can build.
3. **Focus on the First Impression:** Make every interaction count, starting with the first one. Set the tone for a positive, customer-focused experience.
4. **Track Your Process, Not Just Your Results:** Instead of obsessing over PVR, track how consistently you're following your process. Success is about doing the right things consistently.

Summary

The day I stopped obsessing over PVR was the day my career changed. By focusing on the **customer first** and trusting the process, I discovered that the numbers take care of themselves. This mindset isn't just about reducing stress—it's about embracing **servant leadership** and putting the needs of others at the forefront.

When you stop chasing numbers and start focusing on relationships, you'll achieve more than you ever thought possible. **Trust the process, serve your customers, and let your results reflect your commitment to excellence.**

Key Takeaways

1. **Stop chasing numbers**—focus on building trust and providing value.
2. Prioritize relationships over transactions. The numbers will follow.

3. **Master the fundamentals.** Product knowledge, presentation skills, and adaptability are key.
4. Track your process, not just your results. Success is a byproduct of consistency.
5. **Embrace servant leadership.** When you put others first, you create long-term success.

Action Steps

For F&I Managers

1. Set a monthly performance goal and stop checking PVR daily.
2. Focus on creating exceptional first impressions with every customer.

For Dealership Teams

1. Encourage a culture that prioritizes relationships over metrics.
2. Share success stories of team members who've excelled by serving customers first.

For Individual Professionals

1. Practice adapting your approach to different customer personality types.
2. Invest time in improving your product knowledge and presentation skills.

How to Apply This

In the F&I Office

1. Make customer service your top priority. Trust that the results will follow.
2. Regularly review your process and focus on consistency.

Across the Dealership

1. Align your team around the idea that **serving customers comes first.**
2. Celebrate team members who achieve success by building strong relationships.

In Your Daily Practice

1. Start each day with the mindset of serving others, not chasing numbers.

2. Reflect on each interaction and identify ways to improve.

Practical Tools for Success

1. **Monthly Goal Tracker**: Focus on long-term performance, not daily fluctuations.
2. **Process Checklist**: Ensure you're following each step consistently.
3. **Customer Interaction Journal**: Reflect on your interactions to identify strengths and areas for growth.

Reflection Questions

Personal Practice

1. How can I better focus on serving customers instead of chasing numbers?

Resilience

2. What steps can I take to maintain confidence even when metrics fluctuate?

Teamwork

3. How can I encourage my team to prioritize relationships over metrics?

Growth

4. What skills can I develop to better connect with customers and create value?

Bridging Reflection to Action

The numbers will always speak for themselves, but relationships are what truly matter. In the next chapter, we'll explore how to sustain this servant leadership mindset and continue building trust with every customer you serve. Let's lead with service, and the success will follow.

CHAPTER 22:
Advice from the Greats

In this chapter, I am calling on my tribe of automotive mentors to provide thought-provoking advice, inspiring us all to reach greater heights. These incredibly talented individuals answered one pivotal question and shared their all-time favorite quotes to give us something profound to reflect upon. This chapter is as much for me as it is for you, my readers. Enjoy, my friends.

The Balance of Greatness: Humility Meets Hunger

Jonathan Dawson, President, Sellchology

Question: You have trained hundreds of thousands of automotive professionals over your career as a trainer. What separates the average from the exceptional?

Answer: The difference between the average and the exceptional is that the truly exceptional have, often through intentional effort, maintained the delicate balance of humility and hunger. They possess the humility of heart and mind to be coachable and submit to counsel AND the hunger to relentlessly pursue their goals and aspirations!

Humility without hunger makes a person complacent. Hunger without humility makes a person intolerable.

Key Takeaways: The Balance of Greatness—Humility Meets Hunger

The Defining Traits of the Exceptional

1. **Humility:** Exceptional individuals possess the humility to remain open, coachable, and willing to learn from others. They understand the value of counsel and continuously seek improvement.
2. **Hunger:** Equally, they exhibit relentless ambition, pursuing their goals with unwavering determination and passion.

The Danger of Imbalance

1. **Humility Without Hunger:** This leads to complacency, where individuals stagnate, failing to strive for growth and excellence.
2. **Hunger Without Humility:** This approach creates arrogance, making individuals intolerable and difficult to work with, ultimately hindering collaboration and long-term success.

Intentional Effort

1. Achieving greatness requires a conscious commitment to balance humility and hunger. It is not a natural trait but a deliberate practice to sustain personal and professional growth.

A Powerful Perspective

1. True greatness is rooted in the ability to blend a willingness to learn with an unstoppable drive to succeed. Neither trait alone is sufficient; together, they form the foundation of exceptional performance and leadership.

The Myth of the Self-Made Success

Chris Saraceno - Automotive Leader and Mentor, Author of "The Theory of Five"

Question: We know how important personal development is, but unfortunately, many do not have a starting point. What advice would you give an automotive professional who wants to start tipping their toe into becoming a better version of themselves?

Answer: Many individuals in the auto industry claim to be "self-made" or describe others that way. In my view, this is a misconception—a fallacy—as it fails to recognize the significant support and contributions of others that enable success.

The myth of the "self-made" man or woman is just that—a myth. We often admire those who started with little or no resources and went on to build empires. It's tempting to believe they were destined for greatness, achieving success solely through their determination and talent. But when you look closer, you begin to see the people who played pivotal roles in their journey.

There are family and friends who offer encouragement. Teachers and coaches refine skills and help individuals unlock their potential. Trusted mentors guide and inspire greatness. Even doubters play an important role, challenging individuals to prove them wrong and push past their limits.

In this world, we are never truly alone. While some success can be achieved independently, no one reaches their full potential or becomes their best self without the influence of others. Mentors and role models, in particular, are transformative. They don't tell us what to think; they teach us how to think. Through their actions and guidance, they model excellence and inspire results we may not have thought possible.

So, where can you find these mentors and role models? Start by seeking out highly successful automotive professionals who live the kind of career and life you aspire to achieve. Release any envious thoughts like, "They must have known somebody" or "They got lucky." Instead, make an honest assessment of where you are compared to where they are. Many of the people you admire likely started with less than you have now.

Next, ask questions—over and over again. Those who have achieved success are often more than willing to guide and teach someone who approaches them with humility and a willingness to learn. Don't hesitate to ask how they achieved their goals, what habits helped them succeed, and what lessons they've learned.

If you cannot find a mentor locally, there has never been a better time to access virtual mentorship. Online courses, videos, blogs, podcasts, and social media platforms like LinkedIn can connect you with experts worldwide. These tools make it possible to learn from exceptional individuals, even if you're geographically isolated or introverted.

When it comes to personal development, don't just dip your toe in— go all in. Commit fully to your growth and surround yourself with people who elevate you. As the saying goes:

1. "Birds of a feather flock together."
2. "Tell me who your friends are, and I'll tell you who you are."
3. "Iron sharpens iron."

These principles have profoundly impacted my life and the lives of those I've had the privilege to mentor. By embracing mentorship and building a supportive community, you'll create the foundation for transformational personal and professional growth.

Key Takeaways: The Myth of the Self-Made Success

Debunking the "Self-Made" Myth

1. Success is rarely a solo journey; it relies on a network of supporters, mentors, and even doubters who challenge and inspire growth.
2. The idea of being "self-made" overlooks the vital roles that family, friends, and mentors play in shaping personal and professional success.

The Community Behind Success

1. Behind every great achievement is a community of influencers:
    i. **Family and Friends:** Offer encouragement and moral support.
    ii. **Teachers and Coaches:** Refine skills and unlock potential.
    iii. **Mentors:** Provide guidance, challenge thinking, and inspire growth.
    iv. **Doubters:** Spur determination to prove them wrong.

The Transformational Role of Mentorship

1. **What Mentors Do:** They don't tell you what to think but teach you how to think, modeling excellence and providing challenges that inspire growth.
2. **Actions Speak Louder Than Words:** The best mentors lead by example, inspiring results through their behavior.

Finding Mentors and Role Models

1. **Identify Success:** Seek individuals who embody the professional and personal life you aspire to have.
2. **Release Envy:** Avoid assuming their success stems from privilege or luck; recognize their hard work and dedication.
3. **Assess Honestly:** Compare your current state with their achievements to identify areas for growth.

The Power of Asking

1. Saraceno underscores the importance of seeking guidance through intentional questions:
    i. Ask how successful individuals achieved their goals.
    ii. Ask what habits, strategies, and skills were pivotal to their growth.
    iii. Be open to feedback and willing to adapt.

Leveraging Digital Mentorship

1. **Modern Accessibility:** Online platforms like LinkedIn, podcasts, and virtual courses make mentorship accessible to anyone, anywhere.
2. **Lifelong Learning:** Embrace digital tools to continually grow and refine your skills.

Go All in on Personal Growth

1. Half-hearted efforts won't lead to meaningful results. Commit fully to self-improvement by dedicating time and energy to learning and development.
2. Build relationships with growth-oriented individuals to amplify your journey.

Words to Live By

1. Surround yourself with people who elevate you:
     i.   "Birds of a feather flock together."
     ii.   "Tell me who your friends are, and I'll tell you who you are."
     iii. "Iron sharpens iron."

By embracing these principles, you cultivate an environment for profound personal and professional transformation.

The Power of Community and Relationships

Ali Reda – #1 Sales Professional in the World, Les Stanford Chevrolet

Question: You are the number one sales professional in the world. Please tell us, how did you get to where you are today, and can it be replicated by others?

Answer: I can pretty much sum it up in one word: Community! Building relationships that last a lifetime is the cornerstone of my success. People want to do business with people they know, not just know of.

"In our industry, where success is often measured in 30-day increments, my perspective is different. 'I have no beginning; I have no end. My career is not bound by the start and stop of each month. It's continuous. It's a career, not a job.'"

Building a career focused on community and relationships allows for sustainable success that isn't confined to short-term goals. This approach is replicable by others who are willing to shift their mindset and make meaningful connections.

Key Takeaways: The Power of Community and Relationships

The Core Principle

1. **Success Through Community:** Building lasting relationships is the foundation of sustained success. People prefer doing business with those they know and trust rather than acquaintances.

A Long-Term Perspective

1. **Beyond the Monthly Grind:** Viewing your career as a continuous journey rather than a series of 30-day cycles allows for focusing on building deeper, more meaningful connections with clients.
2. **Sustainable Success:** A career-oriented mindset fosters long-term growth, moving beyond short-term goals and into lasting achievements.

Replicable Strategies

1. **Relationship Building:** Focus on genuine interactions and creating trust with clients. This approach leads to customer loyalty and consistent referrals.
2. **Community Engagement:** Embrace your role as a member of your community. Invest in meaningful connections that extend beyond sales transactions.
3. **Mindset Shift:** Adopt the perspective that success is a journey, not a race bound by artificial deadlines like monthly quotas.

When Life Throws the Kitchen Sink at You

Glenn Lundy – Founder 800% Elite Auto Club

Question: When life throws the kitchen sink at you and nothing seems to be going right, what advice would you give that individual?

Answer: Man, when life throws the kitchen sink at you, and it feels like NOTHING is going right, the first thing I'd say is pause and breathe. You're alive, you're still in the fight, and that means there's hope. When everything feels chaotic, sometimes the best thing you can do is step back and remember that storms don't last forever. They never do.

Pause and Breathe: Storms Don't Last Forever

Second, get real about where your focus is. If you're only seeing problems, you're going to find more problems. Shift your focus. Start with gratitude. Even if it feels impossible, write down five things you're thankful for. It could be as simple as the air in your lungs or the roof over your head. Gratitude rewires your mind to start seeing solutions instead of obstacles.

Next, surround yourself with the right people. Isolation is the enemy in tough times. Find your tribe, people who will lift you up, encourage you, and remind you of your worth when you've forgotten. Don't have that circle? Reach out to someone. Join a group. Listen to voices of hope.

And then—TAKE ACTION. It doesn't have to be a big leap. Just one small step in the right direction. Maybe it's making one phone call, sending one email, or simply getting out of bed and showing up for the day. Forward motion creates momentum, and momentum changes lives.

Lastly, lean into faith. Whatever your beliefs are, know there's a bigger picture and a purpose for your pain. Every tough season I've been through has shaped me into the man I am today, and it has prepared me for the blessings that followed. Your storm is refining you, not defining you. Remember that.

So, when the kitchen sink hits you, don't duck and hide. Stand tall, shift your focus, lean into your tribe, take one step, and trust that brighter days are ahead. You've got this. I believe in you.

"We are most comfortable in life right before death."

That quote has always stuck with me because it's a powerful reminder of what comfort means. Comfort is the silent killer of dreams, progress, and impact. It lulls us into complacency, tricking us into thinking we're safe when, really, we're stagnating.

Life isn't meant to be lived in the shallow end. The magic, the growth, the breakthroughs—they all happen in the deep waters, where it's uncomfortable, uncertain, and sometimes even terrifying. So, if you feel uncomfortable right now, good. Lean into it. That's where life truly begins.

Key Takeaway

When life feels overwhelming, find your footing through gratitude, connection, and action. Don't fear discomfort, it's the pathway to transformation. Life is waiting for you in the deep end. Dive in.

Unlocking the Next Level in F&I Success

Joel Kansenback - President, Strategic Dealer Advisory

Question: With your in-depth experience training F&I departments for the past three decades, what is your best advice to an F&I professional who wants to go to the next level?

Answer: Many F&I Managers are held back by limiting beliefs about what's possible in their dealerships. They often feel they're already working as hard as they possibly can, leaving no room for additional effort. However, reaching the next level isn't about working harder—it's about working smarter, being intentional, and enhancing your strategic approach.

To challenge this mindset, I ask a simple but powerful question: "Could you, for 10 deals, run $1,000 higher per retail if the prize was $1 million? And if I gave you 90 days to prepare, what would you do to maximize your chances of winning?"

This hypothetical shifts your perspective, revealing untapped potential and showing you where you can improve.

Here's what you might consider doing to achieve this level of elevated performance:

1. **Spend More Time with Salespeople:** Strengthen relationships and collaboration. A well-prepared sales team creates smoother, more productive F&I transitions.
2. **Tighten Your Menu Presentation:** Ensure every customer interaction is precise, professional, and compelling.
3. **Sharpen Objection Handling:** Practice overcoming objections with finesse, tailoring responses to meet customer needs.
4. **Evaluate Your Office Environment:** Assess whether your office inspires trust and professionalism in customers.
5. **Engage Earlier in Deals:** Get involved sooner to set expectations and establish rapport.
6. **Slow Down and Build Rapport:** A meaningful connection with customers allows for tailored presentations and stronger trust.

7. **Master Lender Programs:** Learn lender programs inside and out to maximize deal potential.
8. **Be Thorough with Cash Deals:** Avoid letting any opportunity slip by treating each deal as unique and essential.

While there won't be a literal $1 million prize in 90 days, following these steps consistently will elevate your performance over time. With a strategic focus, intentional action, and a willingness to push beyond perceived limits, you could achieve earnings that rival—or exceed—that figure.

Quote to Ponder:

"He that is good for making excuses is seldom good for anything else."
— Benjamin Franklin

Key Takeaways: Breaking Through Limiting Beliefs in F&I

Mindset Shifts

1. **Challenge Limiting Beliefs:** Many F&I Managers assume they're already working at full capacity. However, growth comes from working smarter, not harder, and challenging self-imposed limitations.
2. **Adopt a Million-Dollar Perspective**: Reframing challenges as opportunities for significant gains can reveal untapped potential.

Actionable Steps for Elevated Performance

1. **Collaborate With Sales Teams:** Strong relationships with salespeople streamline transitions and create better customer experiences.
2. **Refine Menu Presentations:** Ensure every interaction is professional, precise, and designed to meet customer needs effectively.
3. **Master Objection Handling:** Develop tailored responses to overcome objections with finesse and confidence.
4. **Optimize Office Environment:** A clean, professional space builds customer trust and reinforces credibility.
5. **Engage Early in the Process:** Getting involved sooner allows for rapport building and setting clear expectations with customers.
6. **Build Deeper Customer Connections:** Slowing down and fostering genuine rapport strengthens trust and enhances presentation outcomes.

7. **Leverage Lender Programs:** Understanding lender options thoroughly ensures maximum deal potential.
8. **Focus on Cash Deals:** Treat cash deals with as much attention as financed deals to capture all opportunities.

Path to Long-Term Success

1. **Consistency Over Time:** While no immediate $1 million prize exists, the consistent application of these strategies will yield exceptional results over the long term.
2. **Strategic Focus:** Success requires intentional actions and a willingness to push past perceived limits.

The Core of Compliance: Servant Leadership

Jim Ganther - President, Mosaic

Question: Keeping the dealership compliant is more important than ever before. What is your best advice to a dealer who knows they need to take necessary measures to become compliant but lacks acting in doing so?

Answer: How does a dealer run a compliant operation? The theme of this book, servant leadership, goes a long way toward the answer. Actual compliance is complicated. The desire to be compliant is not, and if you have the latter, the former will surely follow.

A true servant seeks to put the interests of others ahead of their own. This means taking care of a dealership's employees as well as its customers and even the broader community of which it is a part. Let's unpack those categories.

I've never run a dealership, but I do run a company that supports the dealership space. Our employees have flexible workspaces (in-office and remote), site-roasted coffee, and outstanding benefits. We pay top-of-market salaries and allow employees to bring their dogs to work. Our turnover rate is zero.

Why? Simple: If you create work environments and compensation plans that are excellent, your team will work hard to keep those good things. And here's the key takeaway: the easiest way to lose a great job is to oppose leadership's values. The way we treat our employees is the way we expect them to treat our clients.

In other words, it's all about the tone from the top. Talk is cheap. Having written policies that support compliance means nothing if employees see those who cut corners get rewarded. What you tolerate, you encourage. Don't tolerate deceptive trade practices, period. If it's known you will fire a high-performing F&I Manager who packs payments, you can be sure no one else will do it.

This mindset extends to your customers. Is your primary goal serving people with their transportation needs or maximizing profits? Don't get me wrong—there is nothing wrong with making money. It is, in fact, necessary, or your business will fail! But putting profits ahead of serving the customer will eventually eliminate both.

In my prior career as a business litigator, I was always more interested in clients than cases. Clients represent recurring income; cases are one-offs. You create clients by providing both good results and good value.

So, too, in the dealership world. Are you interested in a one-time transaction from an ultimately dissatisfied customer or a repeat customer who sends all her friends and relatives to your store?

Here's a true story to illustrate my point. Victor is a salesman at a large dealer group in the upper Midwest. He is a scary-looking guy: stocky, bald, and with neck tattoos climbing up from his shirt collar to behind his ears. He looks like a homeless drug addict, which he was.

Victor was living in an abandoned car on the streets of Chicago when he had a profound conversion experience. His father, a preacher at a storefront church in Chicago, suggested he sell cars because it was one of the few professions where one could make a decent living without a college degree.

Victor took his father's advice, and in short order, he became the top-selling sales associate at the dealership that took a chance by hiring him. He became the top-selling associate 11 months out of every year. The only month he isn't No. 1 is the month he takes a two-week vacation!

Victor now sells 72 cars every month. The dealership hired an assistant whose only job is to schedule his appointments, so his dance card stays full. Most good sales associates can expect a repeat customer to return every four to five years as the vehicle needs replacement, but Victor's repeat customers start coming in after a week or two. Why? Because his customers tell everyone they know to buy their next car from Victor—and they do.

What makes Victor so special? Simple—he puts his customers' interests ahead of his own. He doesn't just sell; he serves. He will tell customers if the payment on their preferred car will be uncomfortably high and show them more affordable options. People appreciate his sincerity, and not only does he produce amazing volume, but he also holds front-end gross!

Another reason Victor does so well is his "why." Why does he work so hard to humbly serve his customers? To become rich? For an ego boost? Far from it. His goal is to earn enough money to buy his father a proper church building in Chicago. By the time you read this, I suspect he has.

Then, there's service to the community. Examples abound. I live in the Tampa Bay area, and I dare you to find a Little League program that isn't sponsored by the Ferman Motor Car Company. Earlier this year, at a Washington, D.C., Auto Show, I watched DARCARS of Silver Spring donate a dozen Toyotas and complete technician tool kits to local schools to help them train the next generation of auto mechanics. This summer, Bergstrom Automotive contributed $5 for every test drive and $50 for every vehicle sold in June to Make-A-Wish Wisconsin. The donation totaled $355,000.

I could go on, but you get the point—the best dealerships understand that we're all in this together, and those who serve their community will best reap the fruits of gratitude.

Steps to Build a Culture of Compliance

So, there you have it. The way to become compliant is to be committed to service in a compliant manner. The rest is just details, but here are the steps to make compliance a part of your dealership's culture:

Step 1: Leadership's Role in Setting the Tone

Tone from the top is the foundation of compliance. Leadership must embody the values they want to see throughout the organization.

Step 2: The Power of Written Policies

Every dealership must have comprehensive written policies that cover critical areas such as:

1. Sales
2. F&I
3. EH&S/OSHA
4. Privacy Rule
5. Red Flags Rule
6. Safeguards Rule

7. CARS Rule

Step 3: Train, Train, and Train Again

One cannot follow laws they don't know about. Training on the policies and laws impacting every job description must be ongoing.

Step 4: Consistency Is Key

Policies mean little if not followed consistently. Ensure processes are executed as written. For example, filing a FinCEN form 8300 for every qualifying cash transaction must be non-negotiable.

Step 5: Inspect What You Expect

Audit your compliance efforts annually with an independent third party to ensure everything aligns with your policies.

Compliance Is a Heart Issue

Compliance isn't hard if your heart is in it, and if you've got a servant's heart, it will be. Compliance begins and ends with servant leadership—putting others first to ensure the success of the team, the customer, and the community.

Key Takeaways: The Core of Compliance: Servant Leadership

Leadership and Culture

1. **Tone From the Top:** Leadership sets the tone for compliance. Servant leadership, which prioritizes the well-being of employees, customers, and the community, creates a strong foundation for success.
2. **Zero Tolerance:** Rewarding ethical behavior and having no tolerance for cutting corners ensures trust and accountability within the organization.

Employee Engagement

1. **Create a Thriving Workplace:** Offering excellent work environments, benefits, and support encourages employees to align with the dealership's values and treat clients with the same respect and care.
2. **Trust and Relationships:** Employees emulate the treatment they receive from leadership. Strong relationships lead to consistent, ethical practices.

Customer-Centric Approach

1. **Serve Over Sell:** Prioritize customer needs over profits. Customers value sincerity and service, which leads to long-term loyalty and repeat business.
2. **Transparency Matters:** Ethical practices build trust with customers and enhance the dealership's reputation.

Community Engagement

1. **Serve Beyond the Dealership:** Actively participating in and giving back to the community strengthens the dealership's brand and fosters goodwill.
2. **Purpose-Driven Efforts:** When employees and leadership are motivated by a greater purpose, such as community service or personal "whys," it elevates their commitment to excellence.

Steps to Foster a Culture of Compliance

1. **Lead by Example:** Leadership must embody ethical values and set a clear standard for the organization.
2. **Develop Written Policies:** Comprehensive policies covering sales, F&I, safety, and privacy laws provide a framework for consistent operations.
3. **Train Regularly:** Ongoing education ensures employees understand and comply with legal and ethical standards.
4. **Be Consistent:** Policies must be executed consistently across all transactions and processes.
5. **Audit Regularly:** Independent audits ensure compliance is maintained and identify areas for improvement.

Inspiring Examples

1. **Victor's Journey:** Exceptional performance stems from putting customer needs first and staying motivated by a deeper purpose.
2. **Community Impact:** Dealerships that invest in their communities reap the benefits of goodwill and enhanced brand loyalty.

Compliance and Servant Leadership

1. **Heart of Compliance:** True compliance requires a servant's heart—putting the success and well-being of others above self-interest.

2. **Long-Term Success:** Ethical leadership and a service-driven culture lead to sustainable success for the dealership and its community.

The Cornerstone of Greatness: Trust and Relationships in F&I

Rob Ruth – Dealer Principal, Bob Ruth Ford

Question: In your opinion, from a dealer principal's perspective, what makes an F&I department great?

Answer: A great F&I department thrives on a solid foundation of trust and strong relationships. These relationships span across key stakeholders: lenders, employees, the dealer principal, and most importantly, the clients. Trust is not given—it's earned through consistent actions and unwavering integrity over time.

The Long Road to Excellence

Creating a great F&I department doesn't happen overnight. It requires dedication, discipline, and a relentless commitment to doing the right thing. Each action taken by the team, whether it's fostering transparency with lenders or prioritizing the client's needs, contributes to the legacy of trust and excellence.

1. **Lenders:** Establishing trust and open communication with lenders creates smoother transactions and better deal structures.
2. **Employees:** A well-trained, motivated team builds confidence and enhances performance across the dealership.
3. **Clients:** By putting the client first and focusing on their needs, F&I professionals earn loyalty and long-term satisfaction.

Quote to Ponder:

"What you think is what you say. What you say is what you do, and what you do becomes your legacy." — Brandon Dawson

Key Takeaways

1. Trust and relationships are the cornerstone of a successful F&I department.
2. Excellence is built through consistent, value-driven actions over time.
3. A customer-centric approach fosters loyalty, satisfaction, and long-term success.

4. Collaboration with lenders, employees, and clients strengthens the foundation for sustainable growth.

By focusing on trust, relationships, and integrity, F&I departments can deliver exceptional results while creating a lasting impact.

The True Measure of an F&I Turn: Experience Over Time

Josh Potts – GM of the Highest Volume Chevy Store in the Nation

Question: As the GM of the highest volume Chevy store in the nation, what is your expectation on the time length of an F&I turn?

Answer: When it comes to F&I, success isn't measured in minutes but in the quality of the customer experience. The goal is not speed for the sake of efficiency but rather ensuring that the customer leaves satisfied and confident in their decisions. Products and paperwork are only part of the equation; building a relationship and addressing customer questions are equally critical.

The only fixed expectation in the F&I process is that customer interviews are completed immediately upon receiving the deal. From there, the focus shifts to adapting to the customer's unique needs— whether that means taking extra time to answer questions or ensuring clarity in product presentations.

F&I professionals must remain flexible. Some customers may need time to read documents thoroughly or ask additional questions, while others may prefer a quicker transaction. What matters most is that the process is tailored to meet the individual needs of the customer, fostering trust and satisfaction.

Quote to Ponder:

"Light yourself on fire with passion, and people will come from miles away to watch you burn." —John Wesley

Key Takeaways

1. F&I success isn't about rushing—it's about ensuring customer satisfaction.
2. Immediate completion of the customer interview sets the stage for a smooth process.
3. Flexibility and attentiveness create a positive and personalized experience.

4. Building relationships during the F&I turn can lead to long-term loyalty and trust.

By prioritizing the customer's happiness over a rigid timeframe, F&I departments can deliver exceptional value while maintaining efficiency.

Embracing Social Media for Dealership Success

Eric Sanchez Barbosa – Variable Operations Director, Cavender Auto Group

Question: In my opinion, you're one of the top leaders in automotive that has embraced social media. What advice would you give a dealer that knows they need to utilize social platforms but have not taken the steps to do so?

Answer: The digital world is where your audience and customers are already active. To stay relevant, dealerships must embrace this reality. The first step is committing to change—shifting your mindset and operations to meet customers where they are. Social media is no longer optional; it's an essential platform for engagement, communication, and brand-building.

Once the commitment is made, consistency becomes the cornerstone of success. Develop a comprehensive plan and strategy that focuses on consistent engagement. Social media is a marathon, not a sprint. Regular posting, interaction, and adherence to your strategy will cultivate trust and familiarity with your audience.

To make social media efforts sustainable, build a dedicated team or department with clear Key Performance Indicators (KPIs). These KPIs should measure engagement—such as likes, comments, shares, and messages—because engagement is the first step toward generating leads. Over time, those leads will translate into brand awareness and sales.

Rather than solely tracking Return on Investment (ROI), focus on ROE—Return on Engagement. A highly engaged audience is more likely to convert into loyal customers. Engagement fosters connections and strengthens your dealership's brand presence, ultimately driving long-term growth and profitability.

Quote to Ponder:

"Whether you think you can or can't, you're right." —Henry Ford

Key Takeaways

1. Commit to meeting your audience where they are—on social media.
2. Consistency in execution is essential for long-term success.
3. Build a team and track KPIs focused on engagement.
4. Prioritize Return on Engagement (ROE) to build trust, leads, and brand awareness.

By embracing social media with a strategic mindset and consistent execution, dealerships can transform online engagement into tangible business growth. Social platforms are not just tools for advertising; they are powerful channels for creating meaningful connections with customers.

Leading with Purpose and Faith

Mickey Seelye – Dealer Principal, Seelye Auto Group

Question: As a dealer responsible for so many individuals, what is the driving force behind your ability to lead at the highest level?

Answer: As a dealer responsible for so many individuals, the driving force behind my ability to lead at the highest level is doing my best every day to identify my purpose as a leader. When I get it wrong, my priorities drift toward results, performance-based metrics, and how others will view our success.

This mindset places a higher emphasis on *me* rather than *we*.

When I get it right, my priorities shift toward focusing on the leadership gifts, abilities, and opportunities God entrusts me with. This realignment moves my motivation to true servanthood, as though He's the one I'm working for. Ultimately, this leads to more of our team members getting my best.

When I'm able to fully understand my identity is in Christ, the task of giving everything God has blessed me with to others He has placed in my life becomes easier. It ignites the right culture—one that understands what we're responsible for while trusting the results belong to God, who we are serving with our best.

We've found that this culture lowers the pressure, leading to consistently higher performance. When our heart posture is about what we give to others through our work, the results follow naturally.

The only way I could ever see something like this clearly and execute true leadership is through my Lord and Savior, Jesus Christ.

When I accepted Him into my life, I finally understood that success is about how we change the lives of those around us for the better. It's not about us.

Since the scales have been removed from my eyes, I've never had more influence and impact than I do today—and it's all for the glory of God.

Quote to Ponder:

"But someone who does not know, and then does something wrong, will be punished only lightly. When someone has been given much, much will be required in return; and when someone has been entrusted with much, even more will be required." — Luke 12:48 NLT

Key Points:

1. Identifying Purpose as a Leader
2. The Shift Toward Servanthood
3. Finding Identity in Christ
4. Building a Culture of Giving
5. A Transformation Through Faith

From Salesperson to Dealer Principal: A Journey of Growth and Patience

Ken Cook – Dealer Principal, BZ Auto Group

Question: "You worked your way through the ranks to end up where you are today as Dealer Principal. What advice would you give a young salesperson who has dreams of being a dealer someday?"

Answer: My advice for a young salesperson aspiring to become a dealer is twofold. First, understand that every obstacle in your journey is merely a speed bump—not a roadblock or a stop sign.

Treat each challenge as an opportunity to learn and grow rather than viewing it as a barrier to your success. The ability to reframe challenges is what separates those who stagnate from those who excel.

Second, approach everything you do with a sense of urgency. Strive to get things done efficiently and effectively, but balance that drive with patience to allow your efforts to bear fruit over time.

Success is built on relentless forward momentum combined with the wisdom to recognize that growth takes time. You cannot rush greatness, but you must continually move toward it.

1. View obstacles as opportunities for growth.
2. Cultivate a mindset of urgency while respecting the need for patience.
3. Maintain consistent forward momentum in every role you take on.

Quote to Ponder:

"The problem is not that there are problems. The problem is expecting otherwise and thinking that having problems is a problem." — Theodore Isaac Rubin

Maximizing F&I PVR: Strategies for Immediate Impact

Chad Scarberry – Director of Finance, Carousel Auto Group

Question: As a long-time finance director, what is the quickest way to increase F&I PVR in your professional experience?

Answer: The foundation for success starts with having the right people in the organization. Everyone must be aligned with the same objective—from the top leadership to the desk, sales, and F&I. A unified team drives consistent and measurable results.

Consistency is key. Develop a process that can be repeated for every turn. While each store may have its unique traits, the funnel must always lead to the F&I department as the final stage of the transaction.

Matching products to the specific needs of each customer and transaction is vital. Every individual has their own motivations for purchasing, and their experience should feel personalized and relevant to them.

Understanding appropriate pricing is crucial. By breaking down overall goals into smaller segments backed by penetration percentages, you can ensure that pricing strategies align with broader objectives.

Tracking is a cornerstone of growth. Once a goal is set, it must be monitored after every turn. Knowing where you are and where you need to be ensured you're constantly raising the bar.

Strong lending partnerships are essential. Work with lenders who are eager to grow with you. The right lending partner can drive immediate PVR growth.

Training is non-negotiable. Consistent, weekly training helps teams refine their approach, evaluate what went right, and address what went wrong. Success ultimately boils down to excelling in **People, Process, Products, and Pricing.**

Quote to Ponder:

"Gold medals aren't really made of gold. They're made of sweat, determination, and a hard-to-find alloy called guts." — Dan Gable

Unlocking F&I Department Success: Addressing Common Challenges

Preston Stewart – Variable Operations Director, Napleton Auto Group

Question: You have experience running dealerships all over the nation. What is the common theme in an underperforming F&I department?

Answer: Underperforming finance departments consistently grapple with three key challenges:

When comfort breeds complacency, performance stagnates. Teams that are not held accountable or challenged fail to reach their full potential, leading to inefficiencies and missed opportunities.

Training should never be a one-time event. A lack of regular, structured training programs fosters stagnation and prevents teams from adapting to new challenges. Self-discipline among team members is equally critical to ensure they consistently implement learned techniques.

Disconnected sales and finance departments lead to miscommunication, delayed transactions, and a disjointed customer experience. Without seamless synergy, dealerships miss out on maximizing opportunities for profitability and customer satisfaction.

Combat Complacency through Accountability

1. Establish clear performance expectations.
2. Implement regular one-on-one reviews to address gaps and celebrate achievements.

3. Model discipline and drive as a leader to inspire the team.

Reinforce Training as a Cornerstone

1. Prioritize ongoing education through structured programs.
2. Incorporate role-playing, case studies, and consistent follow-ups to solidify learning.
3. Ensure training translates to actionable skills in the real-world environment.

Build Synergy between Sales and Finance

1. Foster open communication and collaboration between sales desks and finance teams.
2. Align goals through daily strategy meetings and joint planning sessions.
3. Emphasize shared accountability to streamline transactions and improve the customer experience.

Key Takeaway:

Realigning these areas isn't an overnight fix. It requires unwavering commitment, consistent effort, and leadership that prioritizes improvement over comfort.

Quote to Ponder:

"If you believe you can or can't, you're right!" — Henry Ford

Marketing Money Missteps: Shifting From Quantity to Quality

Dan Moore – President, Dealer World

Question: You're an expert and a thought leader in the world of marketing and advertising. In today's automotive landscape, where are dealers wasting most of their money in their marketing efforts?

Answer: The majority of dealers' marketing budgets are wasted not because the strategies themselves are ineffective but because they are often deployed to mask deeper operational issues. Instead of addressing these inefficiencies, dealerships pour money into marketing campaigns that attempt to compensate for flawed systems, inadequate training, or outdated processes.

To maximize returns on marketing investments, dealerships should pivot from sheer volume to intentional, data-driven quality. This shift requires a commitment to:

1. **Training the Team:** Equip staff with the skills they need to handle leads effectively and convert inquiries into sales.
2. **Refining Processes:** Streamline customer interactions and sales journeys to reduce friction points and improve experiences.
3. **Embracing Technology:** Adopt tools and platforms that provide measurable insights, enabling targeted marketing efforts that deliver real value.

By addressing these foundational areas, dealers can reduce unnecessary marketing expenditures and focus their budgets on efforts that drive measurable results.

Quote to Ponder:

"A goal without action will forever remain just a dream."

The Power of Data and Storytelling in 2025

Aaron Sheeks – CEO, PureCars

Question: You are the king of data and a blessing to the automotive industry. What changes do you see in the marketplace in 2025 when it comes to utilizing data and acquiring new data?

Answer: The one universal truth, regardless of industry, is that those who tell the story control the narrative. This principle applies not just in families or social circles but also in the world of business. To be a great entrepreneur, you must master the art of storytelling.

Storytelling isn't just a soft skill; it's the foundation of leadership and influence. In the automotive industry, particularly in advertising and sales, this concept becomes even more powerful as we integrate data and automation to shape customer experiences.

By 2025, data will reign supreme in automotive advertising, but it's true potential will only be realized when combined with automation at scale. This combination enables dealerships to create a seamless shopping experience for customers, personalized to their preferences and behaviors.

However, this level of sophistication isn't simple. It demands:

1. **Technological Expertise:** An in-depth understanding of tools and platforms that analyze and utilize data effectively.
2. **Behavioral Insights:** A keen sense of how human behavior evolves at various stages of the customer journey.
3. **Strategic Vision:** The ability to craft cohesive campaigns that merge data with storytelling to guide customers toward action.

Advertising can be summarized as "the ability to manipulate human behavior to drive a specific action or result." When reframed, it aligns with the core principles of leadership and sales:

1. **Leadership:** Seeing life from multiple perspectives and communicating a clear vision others can understand and act upon.
2. **Sales:** Presenting solutions in a way that resonates with customers, inspiring them to take action.

At its heart, this is storytelling. Great leaders and salespeople alike are master storytellers, shaping narratives that drive engagement and action.

The world doesn't wait for anyone, and success belongs to those who act with urgency. Embrace discomfort, face challenges head-on, and sell not just products but hopes and dreams. The future of automotive isn't just about data or technology—it's about the stories we create and the people we inspire.

Quote to Ponder:

"Eat every grenade that life throws at you and sell hopes and dreams to others. Move much faster than you feel comfortable, I'm not sure what you're waiting on."

The Art of Recruitment: Finding and Converting Top Talent

Anthony Santangelo – National Sales Recruiter, AutoMax

Question: As the automotive industry's top sales recruiter, where do you find the most qualified applicants, and what is your approach to converting them to the automotive industry?

Answer: Mastering recruitment begins with mastering the interview process. Just like closing a car deal, interviewing is about understanding the individual's needs, motivations, and potential. It's not a one-size-fits-all approach; you must adapt to each person and see what makes them unique.

The key is to spend adequate time with each candidate, delving into their aspirations, strengths, and values. I approach every interview with the goal of identifying the good in people, seeing their potential, and aligning it with the opportunities in the automotive industry.

1. **Understand Their Needs:** Recruitment isn't about forcing a role onto someone; it's about understanding what they're looking for and aligning it with what the industry can offer.
2. **Adaptability is Key:** Just as no two customers are alike, no two candidates are the same. The ability to adjust your approach for each individual is critical.
3. **Seek the Good in People:** Focus on potential rather than just experience. Many candidates may not come from the automotive world but possess transferable skills that can make them a great fit.

Think of every interview like closing a car deal. You're not just presenting a job; you're presenting a solution that aligns with their aspirations. It's about making them see the automotive industry as a place where they can thrive and grow.

Quote to Ponder:

"If you are waiting to make the perfect decision, you will never make a decision at all." —Tom Selleck

Service Contracts: The Engine that Pulls the Train

Johnny Garlich – President, Heart Dealer Financial Services

Question: I had the honor and privilege to be personally mentored by you for the past two decades. You always instilled in me that the Vehicle Service Contract (VSC) is the engine that pulls the train. What advice would you give an F&I Manager who is underperforming in VSC penetration?

Answer: While F&I Managers have a variety of products that impact a customer's ownership experience, one product transcends all others: the Vehicle Service Contract (VSC). It is the most valuable product for the customer, the dealer, and the F&I Manager.

To fulfill your duty to your dealer, your family, and yourself, you must become an expert in selling service contracts.

Examining F&I sales statistics reveals a strong correlation between service contract sales and other ancillary products. In a menu selling process, if a service contract is sold, the likelihood of selling GAP and other products increases dramatically. *In other words, the service contract sale is the engine that pulls the train for the rest of the products.*

Watching recordings of successful F&I Managers, we consistently observe that when a customer objects to all products, the F&I Manager almost always returns to reaffirming the service contract's value. When the buyer agrees to the service contract, they often agree to additional products if the F&I Manager redirects them to make a menu selection.

Logically, the F&I Manager should sell each product on its own merits. However, using the menu properly allows buyers to focus on one main product. Once the F&I Manager overcomes that objection, the customer frequently selects multiple products. Simply ask the buyer to choose between two menu options that include multiple products. It's the superpower of using a menu: buyers often select several products instead of just one when presented with clear options.

When a finance manager struggles with service contract sales, they usually struggle with their average profit per delivery. If the service contract is the engine pulling the train, fixing weak service contract sales is crucial.

When I ask F&I Managers what they say when customers express disinterest in a service contract, I hear two distinct strategies: one from top-tier F&I Managers and another from those struggling with service contract sales.

Struggling managers often attempt to justify the costs of the car the customer has chosen, emphasizing repair costs and the complexity of modern vehicles. They highlight labor and parts expenses, painting a picture of "computers on wheels" to instill fear in the customer. This "repair scare" strategy suggests the beautiful car they just purchased could lead to frustration and financial strain.

In contrast, top-performing F&I Managers handle objections with a completely different approach. They start by agreeing with the customer. The conversation might look like this:

F&I Manager: "I hear you. When you look at the service contract price of $4,000, you're probably thinking, 'I don't think I'll have $4,000 in repairs. I'd be better off paying for repairs as they happen instead of buying a service contract for $4,000.' Do I have that right?"

Customer: "Yes. I've never spent $4,000 on repairs for any of my Hondas. The service contract doesn't make sense."

F&I Manager: "I get it. When someone says they don't want a service contract, they aren't saying they don't like:

1. Never paying for repairs,
2. Always having a car to drive when their vehicle is in the shop,
3. Avoiding hassle with service techs about what needs to be done or
4. Having a fixed monthly budget.

They love those things. They just feel that, given the initial price of the service contract, they would be better off financially paying for repairs as they happen."

Customer: "Exactly."

F&I Manager: "If you could somehow look into a crystal ball and see that the cost of repairs would exceed the service contract price, would you buy the service contract, enjoy the benefits, and save money? Am I hearing you correctly?"

Customer: "Well... Yes."

F&I Manager: "I don't think you'll have $4,000 in repairs. But our service contract doesn't work the way you think it does. It's designed to save you more than the $4,000 you invest, while ensuring a longer, more reliable, and enjoyable ownership experience. May I show you how it works so you can see if this is a smart financial choice for your family?"

The less successful F&I Manager tries to scare the customer into buying the service contract, going into "fight mode" with their objection. This approach often alienates the customer and creates resistance.

A successful F&I Manager takes the opposite approach. They agree with the customer, restating the objection to validate the customer's concerns. This reframing highlights the service contract's benefits and transitions into a trial close. By asking if the customer would purchase the service contract if they knew it was financially smart, the manager engages the emotional side of the brain. Once the customer's emotions are aligned, the logical side will follow.

One common strategy to reduce the service contract's perceived cost is what I call the "Spreadsheet Close." Here's how it works:

During the initial interview, review the factory warranty and explain that manufacturers budget for repairs during the first 36 months or 36,000 miles.

Ask how many repairs the customer thinks they'll need beyond the bumper-to-bumper warranty. Most customers will say two or three repairs. Even if they only say one, you can demonstrate the math to show the value.

Initial price of a 10-year/150,000-mile service contract: $4,000

A customer plans to keep the car for six years, driving 15,000 miles yearly (a total of 90,000 miles).

Initial cost of VSC: $4,000

Cost of one repair: -$1,600

Cost of VSC after one repair: $2,400

Refund of unused VSC: -$1,600

Net cost of VSC after refund: $800

Higher resale value of the protected car: -$500

Final cost of VSC: $300

Would the customer pay $300 to protect the other 5,999 components of the car, plus receive free rental, towing, and trip interruption? For most, the answer is a resounding "yes."

The key to selling more service contracts is to understand that customers don't want a service contract. They want a reliable car, no budget surprises, and peace of mind. A service contract guarantees that experience.

Some F&I Managers will read this and think it's a great strategy. Others will practice it until it becomes second nature. Those who master this approach will enjoy a rewarding career in the car business. At the end of the day, happy customers who love their cars will drive your success. But you must put in the work.

Good luck. Make this strategy your own. Fit it to your personality. The rewards will follow.

Quote to Ponder:

"Excellence is not a skill. It is an attitude." – Ralph Marston

The collective wisdom of these industry leaders highlights the power of servant leadership, self-awareness, and intentional action. By focusing on building relationships, fostering collaboration, and embracing continuous growth, you can create lasting success. Whether leading an F&I team or striving to grow personally, the principles of service, resilience, and passion pave the way for impact and legacy. I have distilled 30 key takeaways for you to use in your life.

Key Takeaways

Leadership and Mindset

1. **Servant Leadership:** Prioritize serving your employees, customers, and community. True success stems from putting others' needs ahead of your own while maintaining strong values.
2. **Balance Humility and Hunger:** Exceptional leaders are coachable and relentlessly pursue their goals while staying grounded.
3. **Lead by Example:** Actions speak louder than words. Build trust by embodying the behaviors you wish to see in your team.
4. **Focus on Community:** Relationships are the cornerstone of long-term success, creating trust and loyalty that extend beyond short-term goals.

Personal Development

1. **Be Self-Aware:** Confront your limitations, eliminate excuses, and commit to personal growth to unlock your full potential.
2. **Consistency Wins:** Success is built on small, daily habits—whether it's mastering your morning routine, refining your craft, or staying disciplined.
3. **Adaptability Matters:** Embrace change and constantly evolve. The automotive industry (and life) demands flexibility and a willingness to pivot when necessary.
4. **Take Massive Action:** Dreams remain just ideas without execution. Bold, consistent action transforms aspirations into achievements.

Team and Culture Building

1. **Create a Unified Vision:** Align teams across departments—sales, F&I, and service—with shared goals to foster collaboration and efficiency.

2. **Accountability is Key:** Establish clear expectations and hold yourself and your team accountable to maintain high standards.
3. **Nurture Relationships:** Build strong partnerships with lenders, employees, and customers based on trust and shared success.
4. **Elevate Through Training:** Continuous education and development for yourself and your team are non-negotiable for sustained growth.

Sales and F&I Excellence

1. **Master the Art of Persuasion:** Influence with integrity by understanding customer needs and aligning solutions accordingly.
2. **Be Data-Driven:** Use analytics to guide decisions, improve customer experience, and refine strategies.
3. **Early Involvement in Deals:** The earlier F&I is involved, the smoother and more profitable the transaction becomes.
4. **Focus on the Experience:** Move beyond basic service to deliver personalized, memorable interactions for every customer.
5. **Refine Processes:** Great results come from adhering to consistent, well-designed processes that eliminate inefficiencies.

Building Legacy and Impact

1. **Mentorship Shapes Success:** Nobody is truly "self-made." Seek guidance, learn from others, and pay it forward by mentoring the next generation.
2. **Gratitude Fuels Growth:** Cultivate a mindset of gratitude to overcome challenges and build resilience.
3. **Think Long-Term:** Success isn't about hitting one-month goals—it's about building a career and a legacy.
4. **Contribute to the Community:** Impact extends beyond the dealership. Supporting local causes and uplifting others enhances your reputation and influence.

Life Lessons

1. **Lean Into Discomfort:** Growth happens in the uncomfortable, uncertain moments. Embrace challenges as opportunities for breakthroughs.
2. **Resilience is Everything:** When life throws the kitchen sink at you, focus on gratitude, surround yourself with the right people, and keep moving forward.
3. **Own Your Journey:** Every obstacle is a stepping stone. Don't let setbacks define you; let them refine you.

4. **Tell Your Story:** Storytelling is a powerful tool in business and life—it shapes perception, inspires action, and builds connection.

Practical Applications

1. **Hire Right:** Success begins with having the right people in your organization, aligned with the same goals and values.
2. **Trust the Process:** A consistent and repeatable system for F&I and sales ensures results.
3. **Tailor Solutions:** Customize products and experiences to meet specific customer needs.
4. **Track and Measure Success:** Use data and KPIs to continuously improve performance.
5. **Love What You Do:** Passion is contagious. When you're enthusiastic, people want to join your journey and support your vision.

Action Steps

For F&I Managers:

1. Align your team with a shared vision and goals.
2. Integrate F&I earlier into the sales process to maximize opportunities.
3. Use data to refine menu presentations and track performance metrics.

For Dealership Teams

1. Foster trust and collaboration across departments.
2. Implement training programs to keep skills sharp and adaptable.
3. Align operational processes with customer-centric values.

For Individual Professionals

1. Establish a growth-oriented morning routine.
2. Seek mentorship and learn from those who inspire you.
3. Embrace challenges as opportunities for growth and development.

How to Apply This

In the F&I Office

1. Use tailored product offerings to meet customer needs.

2. Maintain transparency and build trust during the transaction process.
3. Track performance metrics to identify areas for improvement.

Across the Dealership

1. Create alignment between sales, F&I, and service through shared goals.
2. Host regular team meetings to encourage collaboration and accountability.
3. Invest in cross-functional training for enhanced team effectiveness.

In Your Daily Practice

1. Prioritize gratitude and reflection to maintain a positive mindset.
2. Leverage feedback to continuously refine your approach.
3. Build meaningful relationships that enhance both personal and professional growth.

Practical Tools for Success

1. **Daily Planner:** Organize priorities and track progress.
2. **Feedback System:** Create a structured process for gathering and applying team insights.
3. **Learning Resources:** Use books, podcasts, and industry reports to stay informed and inspired.

Reflection Questions

Personal Practice

1. How can I cultivate a mindset of gratitude and resilience in my daily life?

Resilience

2. What steps can I take to embrace discomfort as a path to growth?

Teamwork

3. How can I foster stronger collaboration and trust within my team?

Growth

4. What areas of my skill set or knowledge need improvement to reach the next level?

Bridging Reflection to Action

As you absorb these lessons, consider how you'll apply them in your professional journey. Servant leadership demands action, and the next step is creating a personal plan to translate these insights into measurable outcomes.

CHAPTER 23:
Get Out of Your Way

"The greatest obstacle you'll ever face isn't the world outside—it's the limits you place on yourself." — Adam Marburger

Far too often, we find ourselves standing at the crossroads of opportunity and hesitation, held back not by external forces but by the limits we impose upon ourselves. It's easy to point fingers—blaming managers for missed promotions, the economy for financial struggles, or even the weather for a lack of motivation. But here's the truth: **The greatest barrier isn't out there—it's in here.**

The good news? **You have the power to change that.** When you step aside from your own doubts, cultivate self-awareness, and take ownership of your growth, you unlock the ability to lead yourself and others with purpose. In this chapter, we'll explore how to confront your inner obstacles, step boldly into your potential, and inspire those around you to do the same.

The Role of Self-Awareness in Leadership

Self-awareness is the first and most critical step in getting out of your own way. It's the ability to look at yourself honestly—your beliefs, motivations, and behaviors—without judgment.

Ask yourself:

1. Am I holding on to limiting beliefs?
2. Do I allow fear of failure to dictate my decisions?
3. Am I blaming external factors instead of taking responsibility?

When you take the time to reflect, you begin to unravel the patterns and doubts that hold you back. **Self-awareness isn't about finding fault—it's about finding clarity.**

In my own journey, becoming self-aware was one of the toughest yet most rewarding challenges I've faced. It wasn't easy to admit when I was getting in my own way, but that honesty allowed me to grow. It gave me the clarity to make better decisions and lead with confidence.

Servant leadership starts here. When you lead yourself with self-awareness and accountability, you create a foundation for inspiring others to do the same.

Taking Ownership: Stop Pointing Fingers

Blaming others for your struggles might feel satisfying in the moment, but it comes at a cost: **you give away your power to change.** Every time you point fingers; you reinforce the idea that your life is outside your control. True growth begins when you take ownership of your choices and outcomes.

Here's the reality:

1. Your past doesn't define your future.
2. Every setback is an opportunity to learn.
3. Every failure is a stepping stone to success.

As a servant leader, taking ownership isn't just about personal growth—it's about empowering others to take ownership of their lives as well. **When you lead with accountability, you set an example for your team, your family, and your community.**

Embracing Discomfort: The Path to Growth

Growth isn't supposed to feel easy. It's uncomfortable, messy, and full of uncertainty. But here's the thing: **discomfort is where transformation happens.**

If you wait for the perfect moment or ideal conditions, you'll stay stuck. Success comes to those who step into the unknown, take risks, and embrace the challenges along the way.

Action transforms potential into reality. The moment you stop waiting and start doing, you begin to rewrite your story. And as you do, you inspire others to take their own bold steps forward.

Remember: It's not your circumstances that define you—it's how you respond to them.

Practical Exercises to Cultivate Self-Awareness

Self-awareness isn't just a concept—it's a practice. Here are eight exercises to help you uncover what's holding you back and move forward with clarity:

1. Daily Reflection Journal

1. **Exercise**: Spend 10–15 minutes each day reflecting on your thoughts, emotions, and actions. Use prompts like:
   i. What went well today?
   ii. What didn't go well, and why?
   iii. How did I react to challenges?
2. **Purpose**: Identify patterns in your behavior and emotional responses to better understand yourself.

2. Mindfulness Meditation

1. **Exercise**: Dedicate a few minutes daily to mindfulness. Focus on your breath and observe your thoughts without judgment.
2. **Purpose**: Build presence and awareness, allowing you to respond thoughtfully rather than react impulsively.

3. Feedback Loop

1. **Exercise**: Ask trusted colleagues or friends for constructive feedback on your strengths and areas for improvement.
2. **Purpose**: Gain external perspectives to uncover blind spots and accelerate your growth.

4. Strengths and Weaknesses Analysis

1. **Exercise**: Create a list of your strengths and weaknesses. Reflect on how they influence your personal and professional life.
2. **Purpose**: Leverage your strengths while addressing areas for growth.

5. Visualization of Goals

1. **Exercise**: Picture where you want to be in five or ten years. Write down the steps to get there and the barriers you need to overcome.
2. **Purpose**: Gain clarity on your aspirations and take actionable steps toward achieving them.

Your Tribe of Mentors

One of the most transformative lessons I've learned came from my former MMA coach, Jesse Finney. He used to say, **"Show me your friends, and I'll show you your future."** At the time, I didn't fully understand it, but as I've grown, I've realized how true it is: **the people you surround yourself with shape your trajectory.**

If you spend your time with people who challenge you, support you, and inspire you to grow, you'll elevate. But if you surround yourself with people who settle for mediocrity, you'll find yourself stuck there, too.

Here are key questions to evaluate your inner circle:

1. Does this person pour positive energy into my life?
2. Do they challenge me to grow?
3. Are they genuinely invested in my success?
4. Do they hold me accountable?
5. Are they winning in their own lives?

If the answer to these questions is "no," it might be time to distance yourself. Not everyone is meant to sit at your table—and that's okay.

Organizing Your Tribe: The Bucket System

To better manage your relationships, I recommend categorizing them into the following buckets:

Bucket A:

Your closest relationships—spouse, children, business partners, and closest friends who align with your vision and goals.

Bucket B:

Friends and colleagues who wish you well but aren't actively involved in your growth journey.

Bucket C:

Friends who are fun to be around but lack growth-oriented mindsets. These relationships should have limited time investment.

Bucket D:

Acquaintances or casual connections who play a minor role in your life.

Bucket F:

The "F You" bucket—those who've wronged or betrayed you. While it's crucial to forgive them, it's equally important to set boundaries and move forward.

Summary

The greatest obstacle you'll ever face isn't the world around you—it's you. But here's the good news: **you have the power to step out of your own way.** By cultivating self-awareness, taking ownership of your life, and surrounding yourself with the right people, you can unlock your potential and lead a more fulfilling, purpose-driven life.

Key Takeaways

1. **You are your greatest obstacle.** Stop blaming external factors and take responsibility for your growth.
2. **Self-awareness is key.** Reflect on your thoughts and actions to uncover what's holding you back.
3. **Surround yourself with winners.** The people you spend time with shape your future.
4. **Growth requires discomfort.** Embrace challenges as opportunities to grow.
5. **Lead yourself first.** Servant leadership begins with personal accountability and growth.

Action Steps

For F&I Managers

1. Spend time each day reflecting on how your decisions impact your team.
2. Lead by example—show your team the value of self-awareness and accountability.

For Dealership Teams

1. Foster a culture of self-awareness by encouraging open feedback and reflection.
2. Celebrate team members who take ownership of their growth.

For Individual Professionals

1. Begin a daily reflection journal to identify limiting beliefs.

2. Evaluate your inner circle and prioritize relationships that inspire and challenge you.

Practical Tools for Success

1. **Reflection Journal**: Track your thoughts, emotions, and behaviors daily.
2. **Tribe Evaluation Worksheet**: Organize your relationships into buckets and identify where changes are needed.
3. **Feedback Checklist**: Seek input from trusted individuals to uncover blind spots.

Bridging Reflection to Action

Getting out of your own way starts with self-awareness, accountability, and surrounding yourself with the right people. It's not an easy journey, but it's one worth taking. The next step is yours—take it boldly. The world is waiting for you to lead.

CHAPTER 24:
Go Out into the World and Take What's Yours

"The road ahead may be filled with challenges, but it is also paved with endless possibilities. Go out and take what's yours." — Adam Marburger

As we reach the conclusion of this journey together, I want you to pause and reflect on the path we've traveled. The automotive industry is not just a collection of vehicles, engines, and technologies; it is a **vibrant ecosystem bursting with potential, opportunities, and transformation.**

This industry offers the tools to turn your dreams into reality—but only if you're willing to take action. The lessons and insights we've explored in this book are not just words on a page; they are tools meant to empower you. **The key to unlocking your future is action.**

Action: The Bridge Between Dreams and Reality

We all have brilliant ideas—concepts that could transform our careers and lives. Yet, too often, those ideas wither away because we fail to act. We sit idly, wondering why success seems to skip over us. But here's the truth: **action is the bridge that connects dreams to reality.**

You owe it to yourself, your family, and the younger generation looking up to you to take that action. Each step you take sets an example for others. **Servant leaders understand that their actions inspire those who follow.**

I remember a time early in my career when I hesitated to propose a new strategy to my team. I feared rejection or failure. But I finally decided to act—and that decision not only led to a boost in revenue but also inspired my team to take ownership of their roles. That single moment showed me the power of massive action.

Lesson: Success doesn't come to those who wait. It comes to those who act.

Plant the Seeds of Success

The knowledge you've gained from this book is not meant to sit idle. **It's meant to be planted, nurtured, and turned into growth.** Don't let these lessons die on the vine. Take what you've learned and put it into action—today.

Challenge yourself

1. Step outside your comfort zone.
2. Pursue growth personally and professionally.
3. Take massive action because massive action breeds massive results.

Yes, it will be uncomfortable at first. Growth always is. But it is through discomfort that we achieve greatness. **Remember, the world doesn't reward the idle—it rewards the bold.**

Servant Leadership: Leading by Example

As you continue this automotive journey, know this: your leadership has the power to transform not just your life but the lives of those around you. **Servant leadership is about using your growth to inspire and elevate others.**

Every action you take serves as an example to your team, your family, and your community. By stepping into your potential, you empower others to do the same. **You show them that with hard work, courage, and perseverance, success is possible.**

Lessons from a Life in Automotive

Reflecting on my own journey, I can't help but feel gratitude for the opportunities this industry has given me. The automotive world has taught me everything I needed to succeed in life:

1. **Communication skills**: I learned how to connect with people effectively, which now allows me to speak to audiences nationwide.
2. **Financial acumen**: The F&I office taught me accounting and money management, skills I use every day in my operations.

3. **Lifelong relationships**: Over the past two decades, I've had the privilege of working with some of the greatest people I've ever known.

I'm a college dropout who found my purpose in automotive. This industry gave me more than a career—it gave me a life.

I share this with you because I want you to know that if I can do it, so can you. Whatever your background or circumstances, this industry is full of possibilities. The skills you gain here can unlock doors you never imagined.

Summary

The greatest obstacle you'll ever face isn't the world around you—it's you. But here's the good news: **you have the power to step out of your own way.** By cultivating self-awareness, taking ownership of your life, and surrounding yourself with the right people, you can unlock your potential and lead a more fulfilling, purpose-driven life.

Key Takeaways

1. **Action is everything.** Dreams become reality only when you take the steps to make them happen.
2. **You are an example.** Every action you take inspires others to believe in their potential.
3. **Servant leaders act boldly.** Your growth empowers those you lead.
4. **The automotive industry is full of possibilities.** The skills you gain here can transform your life.
5. **Massive action breeds massive results.** The universe rewards those who show up and do the work.

Action Steps

For F&I Managers

1. Spend time each day reflecting on how your decisions impact your team.
2. Lead by example—show your team the value of self-awareness and accountability.

For Dealership Teams

1. Foster a culture of self-awareness by encouraging open feedback and reflection.
2. Celebrate team members who take ownership of their growth.

For Individual Professionals

1. Begin a daily reflection journal to identify limiting beliefs.
2. Evaluate your inner circle and prioritize relationships that inspire and challenge you.

How to Apply This

In the F&I Office

1. Use the lessons you've learned to take ownership of every opportunity and challenge.
2. Encourage collaboration by leading with gratitude and action.

Across the Dealership

1. Promote a culture of massive action by celebrating bold decisions and growth-oriented efforts.
2. Align your team's goals with a shared sense of purpose and vision.

In Your Daily Practice

1. Reflect daily on the actions you've taken and the results you've achieved.
2. Use gratitude as a guiding principle to inspire yourself and those around you.

Practical Tools for Success

1. **Reflection Journal**: Track your thoughts, emotions, and behaviors daily to gain clarity and focus.
2. **Goal Mapping Worksheet**: Outline bold goals and the steps needed to achieve them.
3. **Team Gratitude Sessions**: Foster a culture of positivity and accountability by celebrating small and large wins.

Reflection Questions

Personal Practice

1. What bold goal can I pursue today to take ownership of my growth?

Resilience

2. How will I respond to challenges with determination and positivity?

Teamwork

3. How can I inspire my team to act with purpose and gratitude?

Growth

4. What habits can I build to stay consistent in my pursuit of massive action?

Bridging Reflection to Action

The lessons in this book are only as powerful as the actions you take to implement them. **The world is yours for the taking—but it's up to you to go out and claim it.** Take massive action today and watch as your life transforms.

FINAL NOTE FROM ADAM

Thank you for spending this time with me. It has been an honor and a privilege to share my journey with you. My hope is you found some value in my writings and you're able to make positive impact in your personal and professional life. As you continue in your automotive journey, always be looking to lend a hand to the younger generation.

I wish you all nothing but the best.

Remember: The universe favors gratitude and action.

Your friend in automotive, Adam

TRAINING CAMP WITH ADAM MARBURGER

The Next Chapter in F&I Excellence

As you close this chapter of learning, I'd like to invite you to continue growing alongside me through *Training Camp with Adam Marburger*. This exclusive series on CBT News brings together the industry's brightest minds, offering actionable strategies, leadership insights, and innovative approaches to F&I management.

Training Camp was created to fill a gap in the automotive world—a lack of consistent mentorship and training that addresses the unique challenges of margin compression, compliance, and evolving customer expectations. Each episode is designed to empower professionals to excel in the four pillars of F&I success: transactional mastery, customer connection, operational efficiency, and compliance.

In *Training Camp*, I share my own journey and the tools that have helped me, and countless others thrive, from my F&I Blackbelt Process to lessons learned from industry thought leaders. Together, we explore how the principles of preparation, discipline, and servant leadership can transform careers and organizations.

The fight is never won in the moment; it's won in the preparation. Whether it's on the mats of Brazilian Jiu-Jitsu or in the high-stakes environment of F&I, the work you do behind the scenes defines your victories. Join me in *Training Camp* to continue honing your skills, building resilience, and mastering the art of leadership.

You can find *Training Camp with Adam Marburger* on CBT News or explore more resources at AdamMarburger.com.

Thank you for being part of this journey. I look forward to seeing how you apply these principles to create success for yourself and those around you.

ABOUT THE AUTHOR

Adam Marburger is a trailblazing entrepreneur, transformational leader, and renowned coach with over 20 years of experience redefining leadership in the automotive and financial services industries. As President and CEO of **Ascent Dealer Services**, Adam has helped dealerships nationwide achieve record-breaking growth through his innovative strategies and **Best-in-Class F&I products**. His commitment to excellence and dedication to servant leadership have set him apart as a respected voice in the industry.

A **black belt in Brazilian Jiu-Jitsu**, Adam's passion for discipline and resilience extends beyond business. He owns **Alton Family Martial Arts & Fitness**, where he empowers individuals to grow mentally, physically, and emotionally. His drive to uplift others also inspired the creation of **Riverbend Rescue**, a nonprofit supporting underprivileged youth in his community.

Adam is also a best-selling author. His books, including *You're the F*cking Problem: A Guide to Getting Out of Your Own Way* and *The Servant-Leading F&I Manager: Leadership Redefined,* challenge readers to embrace accountability, redefine leadership, and achieve personal and professional success. Through his writing, Adam equips leaders with the tools to inspire, serve, and lead with integrity.

As a dynamic speaker and trainer, Adam captivates audiences with his authentic and results-driven approach to leadership. From keynote speeches to hands-on workshops, Adam's engaging style and actionable strategies motivate and equip participants to transform their teams and organizations. Whether addressing a room of executives or training frontline managers, Adam delivers unparalleled insights that drive real-world success.

When not leading businesses or inspiring others, Adam treasures time with his three daughters—Ahnalee, Arabelle, and Astyn—who remain his greatest source of joy and motivation. Through his words and actions, Adam exemplifies the power of servant leadership, transforming not just businesses but lives.

WORK WITH ADAM

Are you ready to transform your team, elevate your leadership, and achieve unprecedented results? Adam Marburger is here to help you take your organization and career to the next level.

With his proven approach to servant leadership, Adam offers:

- **Best-in-Class F&I Products and Solutions:** Drive profitability and success with Ascent Dealer Services' premier offerings.
- **Tailored Coaching Programs:** Receive actionable insights and strategies designed specifically for your business.
- **Dynamic Speaking Engagements:** Inspire and energize your team with Adam's practical and motivational talks.
- **Leadership Training Workshops:** Equip your leaders with tools to drive performance, foster growth, and build winning teams.
- **Strategic Consulting:** Unlock new levels of performance and profitability with customized solutions.

CONTACT ADAM TODAY

Email: adam.marburger@ascentdealerservices.com

Phone: (618) 979-9483

Web:

www.adammarburger.com

www.ascentdealerservices.com

Facebook: www.facebook.com/adammarburger

LinkedIn: www.linkedin.com/in/adam-marburger/

Instagram: www.instagram.com/adampmarburger/

Training Camp:

www.youtube.com/playlist?list=PLXuDpV5qMyCJfiE4v-wJSrZOvDc0DA9du

YouTube: www.youtube.com/@adammarburger2495

Linktree: www.linktr.ee/AdamPMarburger

Transform your team. Elevate your leadership. Book Adam for your next event, training session, or to explore Best-in-Class F&I products today!

www.ingramcontent.com/pod-product-compliance
Lightning Source LLC
Chambersburg PA
CBHW060545200326
41521CB00007B/496